Learning to Pass

New CLAiT 2006

e-publication creation

Unit 4

Ruksana Patel

www.heinemann.co.uk
✓ Free online support
✓ Useful weblinks
✓ 24 hour online ordering

01865 888058

D0332441

Heinemann

Inspiring generations

Heinemann Educational Publishers
Halley Court, Jordan Hill, Oxford OX2 8EJ
Part of Harcourt Education

Heinemann is the registered trademark of Harcourt Education Limited

Text © Ruksana Patel 2006

First published 2006

10 09 08 07 06
10 9 8 7 6 5 4 3 2 1

British Library Cataloguing in Publication Data is available
from the British Library on request.

10-digit ISBN: 0 435 08264 7
13-digit ISBN: 978 0 43508264 2

Typeset by TechType, Abingdon, Oxon

Original illustrations © Harcourt Education Limited, 2006

Cover design by Wooden Ark

Printed in the UK by Bath Colour

Cover photo © Getty Images

Acknowledgements
Every effort has been made to contact copyright holders of material reproduced
in this book. Any omissions will be rectified in subsequent printings if notice is
given to the publishers.

The author would like to thank Abdul Patel for working through the book and
proofs and for his support, patience and invaluable feedback during the writing
of this series. Thank you to Stephe and Mur Cove for their invaluable feedback.
Thank you to Fayaz and Fozia Roked and Penny Hill for their support. Thank you
to Lewis Birchon and Gavin Fidler for their invaluable input which has improved
the quality of the book and for their constant support, advice and patience
during the production process.

Microsoft product screenshots reprinted with permission from Microsoft
corporation.

Tel: 01865 888058   www.heinemann.co.uk

Contents

More general advice on preparation for the assessment and the Definition of terms can be found on the CD-ROM that accompanies this book.

Introduction to New CLAiT

This book has been designed to cover the syllabus for Unit 4: e-publication creation of the OCR Level 1 Certificate/Diploma for IT Users (New CLAiT).

Structure of the qualification

UNIT STATUS	UNIT TITLE
Core unit	Unit 1: File management and e-document production
Optional units	Unit 2: Creating spreadsheets and graphs
	Unit 3: Database manipulation
	Unit 4: e-publication creation
	Unit 5: Create an e-presentation
	Unit 6: e-image creation
	Unit 7: Web page creation
	Unit 8: Online communication
	Unit 9: Computing fundamentals (IC^3)
	Unit 10: Key applications (IC^3)
	Unit 11: Living online (IC^3)

All units are equally weighted. Candidates may work towards the units in any particular order and learning programmes can be tailored to meet individual needs.

Learning outcomes for Unit 4: e-publication creation

A candidate following a programme of learning leading to this unit will be able to:

- identify and use appropriate software correctly in accordance with laws and guidelines
- use basic file handling techniques for the software
- set up a standard page layout and text properties
- use basic tools and techniques appropriately
- import and place text and image files
- manipulate text and images to balance a page
- manage publications and print composite publications.

Guided learning hours

An average candidate should take around 20 guided learning hours per unit to acquire the knowledge, understanding and skills necessary to pass that unit. However, this figure is for guidance only and will vary depending on individual candidates and the mode of learning.

Assessment

Units 1 to 8 are assessed in a centre by a centre assessor and are then externally moderated by an OCR examiner-moderator. OCR sets the assessments. Candidates are allowed a notional duration of $2\frac{1}{2}$ hours for each assessment. If candidates do not pass an OCR-set assignment at the first attempt, they may have other attempts at a unit using a different OCR-set assignment. In order to achieve a unit pass, candidates must make no critical errors and no more than four accuracy errors. For detailed marking criteria please refer to the OCR Level 1 Certificate/Diploma for IT Users (New CLAiT) Tutor's Handbook.

Certification

Candidates may achieve individual unit certificates, an OCR Level 1 Certificate for IT Users (New CLAiT) or an OCR Level 1 Diploma for IT Users (New CLAiT). Each unit is regarded as a worthwhile achievement in its own right. Candidates have the option of achieving as many or as few units as are appropriate. Candidates will be awarded a unit certificate for each individual unit achieved.

To achieve the Level 1 Certificate for IT Users qualification, candidates are required to achieve **three** units including the core unit (Unit 1). Candidates who achieve **five** units, including the core unit (Unit 1), will be awarded an OCR Level 1 Diploma for IT Users (New CLAiT).

Progression

Candidates who are successful in achieving accreditation at Level 1 will be able to progress to the OCR Level 2 Certificate/Diploma for IT Users. New CLAiT also provides a basis for progression to the NVQs which form part of the ITQ suite, NVQ Levels 1, 2 and 3 for IT Users.

The ITQ qualification

The ITQ is a flexible IT user qualification and training package that can be tailored to ensure you are trained in the IT skills that you need for your job. The ITQ is the new NVQ for IT Users. It forms part of the new Apprenticeship Framework for IT Users and it has been bench-marked against the e-skills National Occupational Standards.

New CLAiT 2006 and the ITQ

New CLAiT 2006 can contribute towards the ITQ qualification and the table below shows how New CLAiT 2006 maps against the ITQ. All required ITQ knowledge and skills content is covered in the New CLAiT 2006 units and the CLAiT assessment fully meets the requirements of the assessment strategy for the e-skills UK qualification.

E-SKILLS UK UNITS	NEW CLAIT UNITS
Operate a computer 1 (OPU1)	Unit 1 File management and e-document production
Word processing 1 (WP1)	Unit 4 e-publication creation
Spreadsheet software 1 (SS1)	Unit 2 Creating spreadsheets and graphs
Database software 1 (DB1)	Unit 3 Database manipulation
E-mail 1 (MAIL1)	Unit 8 Online communication
Presentation software (PS1)	Unit 5 Create an e-presentation
Website software 1 (WEB1)	Unit 7 Web page creation
Artwork and imaging software 1 (ART1)	Unit 6 e-image creation

This book covers the syllabus for WP1: Word processing of the ITQ at Level 1. You can use other units from New CLAiT 2006 and CLAiT Plus 2006 (which are published in Heinemann's *Learning to Pass New CLAiT/CLAiT Plus* 2006 series) as well as other qualifications to count towards your ITQ.

Therefore, if you are embarking on the ITQ and you have selected this unit then this book will ensure that you have the knowledge and skills required to successfully complete the unit.

The ITQ Calculator and e-skills Passport

The ITQ can be achieved at three levels and each of the units has points allocated to them so all the units together should add up to the total necessary for the level required. The table on the next page gives you the unit values so that you can see how an ITQ can be built for the level you are aiming to achieve. You can take units from different levels in order to achieve the desired number of points. However, if you aim to achieve the ITQ then you must take the mandatory unit (Make selective use of IT) and at least 60% of your unit choices must be at the ITQ level that you wish to achieve.

E-Skills UK has created the e-skills Passport, an online tool, which helps you build your IT User skills profile. It is not a qualification, nor is it a formal appraisal system, but it is a means to steer you towards the right mix of training and/or qualifications that suit you and your employer. For more information visit the e-Skills UK website (www.e-skills.com).

	ITQ LEVELS		
	Level 1	Level 2	Level 3
Total required	40	100	180
Total of points to come from optional units at level of qualification	15	40	75

Who this book is suitable for:

This book is suitable for:

- anyone working towards:
  - OCR Level 1 Certificate/Diploma for IT Users (New CLAiT)
- a complete beginner, as no prior knowledge of Publisher is required
- use as a self-study workbook – the user should work through the book from start to finish
- tutor-assisted workshops or tutor-led groups
- anyone wanting to learn to use Microsoft Office Publisher 2003. Default settings are assumed.

Although this book is based on Publisher 2003, it may also be suitable for users of Microsoft Publisher 2002 (XP). Note that some features will be different and some screen prints will not be identical.

UNIT 4: e-publication creation

How to use this book

In Unit 4: e-publication creation, you will need to create a single-page publication. The publication will contain text and images arranged in columns.

This book is divided into three sections:

- ○ in Section 1, you will learn how to set up the page layout, create text boxes, enter and format text
- ○ in Section 2, you will learn how to insert text files and images and print a publication
- ○ in Section 3, you will learn how to make changes to text and images, draw shapes and finalise the publication.

You will use a software program called Microsoft Office Publisher 2003 which is part of Microsoft Office. We will refer to it as Publisher from now on. Publisher is a desktop publishing program that can be used to create a variety of publications in various formats. It has desktop publishing features (e.g. text flow, image control) that are more advanced than a word-processing package.

How to work through this book

1 Before you begin this unit, make sure that you feel confident with the basics of using a computer and Windows XP. These skills are covered in Chapter 1 of the Unit 1 book, *Learning to Pass New CLAiT: File management and e-document production*.

2 Read the explanation of a term first.

3 If there are some terms you do not understand, refer to the Definition of terms.

4 Work through the book in sequence so that one skill is understood before moving on to the next. This ensures understanding of the topic and prevents mistakes.

5 Read the ▶▶ *How to...* guidelines which give step-by-step instructions for each skill. Do not attempt to work through the How to... guidelines. Read through each point and look at the screenshots. Make sure that you understand all the instructions before moving on.

6 To make sure that you have understood how to perform a skill, work through the Check your understanding task following that skill. You should refer to the How to... guidelines when doing the task.

7 At the end of each section is an Assess your skills table. Read through these lists to find out how confident you feel about the skills that you have learned.

8 Towards the end of the book there are **Quick reference guides**, **Build-up** and **Practice tasks**. Work through each of the tasks.

If you need help, you may refer to the How to… guidelines or Quick reference guides while doing the Build-up tasks. While working on the Practice tasks, you should feel confident enough to only use the Quick reference guides if you need support. These guides may also be used during an assessment.

A CD-ROM accompanies this book. On it are the files that you will need to use for the tasks. Instructions for copying the files are given below. The solutions for all the tasks can be found on the CD-ROM in a folder called **publications_workedcopies**.

Note: there are many ways of performing the skills covered in this book. This book will provide How to… guidelines that have proven to be easily understood by learners.

Files for this book

To work through the tasks in this book, you will need the files from the folder called **files_publications**. This folder is on the CD-ROM provided with this book. Copy this folder into your user area before you begin.

▶▶ How to... *copy the folder files_publications from the CD-ROM*

Make sure the computer is switched on and the Desktop screen is displayed.

1 Insert the CD-ROM into the CD-ROM drive of your computer.

2 Close any windows that may open.

3 On the Desktop, double-click on the **My Computer** icon.

4 The **My Computer** window will be displayed.

5 Under **Devices with Removable Storage**, double-click on the **CD Drive** icon to view the contents of the CD-ROM.

6 A window displaying the contents of the CD-ROM will appear.

7 Double-click on the folder **L1_Unit 4_Pubn** to open the folder.

8 Click once on the folder **files_publications** (Figure 1). The folder will be highlighted (usually in blue).

FIGURE 1 The contents of the folder

9   In the **File and Folder Tasks** section, click on **Copy this folder**.

10   The **Copy Items** dialogue box will be displayed (Figure 2).

11   In this window, click on the user area where you want to copy the folder **files_publications** to.

12   Click on **Copy**.

13   The folder **files_publications** will be copied to your user area.

FIGURE 2 The Copy Items dialogue box

What does it mean?

User area

A user area is the workspace on a computer where you will save your files. One example of a user area is a folder called My Documents; Windows XP creates this area. In a centre, you may be given a work area on a network. This area may have a drive name (e.g. G drive). Or you may save your work on a floppy disk, which is usually the A drive. On your own personal computer, your user area may be the My Documents folder.

TIP!

Paste a second copy to another folder in your user area as backup.

How to use the keyboard to enter data

HOW TO...	ACTION
Type one capital letter	Hold down the **Shift** key and press the required letter on the keyboard then let go of the Shift key
Type word(s) in capital letters	Press down the **Caps Lock** key
Type lower-case letters	Check the **Caps Lock** key is switched off
Insert a space between words	Press the **spacebar** once
Delete a letter to the left of the cursor	Press the **Backspace** key
Delete a letter to the right of the cursor	Press the **Delete** key

When you enter text, make sure you use the same case as shown.

CASE	EXAMPLE
lower case	this text is in lower case
Initial Capitals	Each Of These Words Has An Initial Capital
UPPER CASE	THIS TEXT IS IN UPPER CASE

When you enter text, make sure you use the *correct spacing* – **one space between each word**.

Section 1: Create a publication

In this section you will learn how to:

- start Publisher and understand the Publisher window
- understand and use the Master Page
- set the page size and orientation
- save a publication
- set the margins
- insert headers and footers
- close a publication
- open a publication (from within Publisher and from My Computer)
- understand publication page layout
- understand and create text boxes
- use the zoom tools
- adjust the height or width of a text box
- set the text box margins
- enter a heading
- highlight text
- differentiate between serif and sans serif fonts
- format the font
- format the font size
- set the character spacing (kerning)
- set up columns in a text box
- display column guides.

Starting Publisher

▶▶ How to... *start Publisher*

1 Click on the **Start** button.

2 Click on **All Programs**.

3 Click on **Microsoft Office**.

4 Click on **Microsoft Office Publisher 2003**.

5 Publisher will open with a task pane on the left of the screen.

6 Click on the cross to the right of **New Publication** to close the task pane (Figure 4.1).

7 A blank page titled **Publication1** will be displayed.

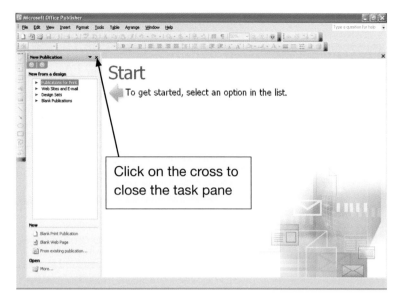

Click on the cross to close the task pane

FIGURE 4.1 Closing the task pane

Start Publisher

1 Start Publisher.

2 Close the task pane.

3 A blank publication titled **Publication1** will be displayed. Keep the blank publication open.

Getting familiar with the Publisher window

Figure 4.2 shows the various components of the Publisher window.

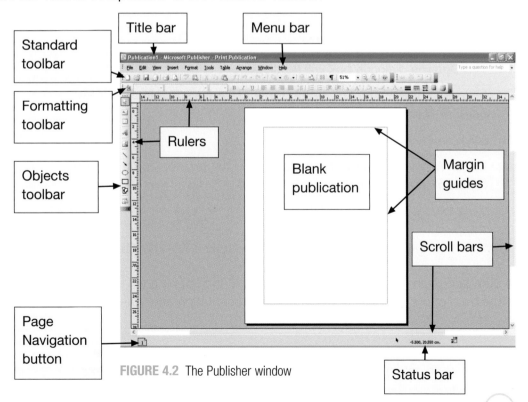

Title bar

Menu bar

Standard toolbar

Formatting toolbar

Rulers

Objects toolbar

Blank publication

Margin guides

Scroll bars

Page Navigation button

FIGURE 4.2 The Publisher window

Status bar

Take a few minutes to learn the different parts of Publisher.

FEATURE	ACTION
Title bar	Displays the name of the current publication (**Publication1**), the name of the program (**Microsoft Publisher**) and the type of publication (**Print Publication**)
Menu bar	A list of options. Click on a menu item to see the drop-down menu
Standard toolbar	Includes icons for commonly used tasks (e.g. Save, Print)
Formatting toolbar	Includes icons for commonly used formatting for text (e.g. bold, centre). The icons are ghosted (pale grey) if the publication is blank or if a text box is not selected
Objects toolbar	Displays icons used to create objects on a page (e.g. text box, picture frame)
Blank publication	The main publication in the centre of the screen
Status bar	Displays the number of pages in a publication and the position and size of objects
Margin guides	The blue borders within the publication
Rulers	Horizontal and vertical rulers are displayed. Rulers help position objects accurately in a publication
Page Navigation button	Displays the current page number $\boxed{1}$ in the publication or displays as $\boxed{A}$ in Master Page view

▶▶ How to... *set the option to close the task pane (optional)*

1 Click on the **Tools** menu.

2 Click on **Options**.

3 The **Options** dialogue box will be displayed.

4 Make sure there is no tick in the box for **Use New Publication task pane at startup**.

5 Click on the **User Assistance** tab.

6 Under Wizards, click to remove the tick in the box for **Use a Wizard for blank publications**.

7 Click **OK**.

Understanding the Master Page (template)

A standard page layout is set up to ensure that the appearance of all pages in a publication is consistent (e.g. the orientation and margins of all pages in a publication will be the same).

In Publisher the Master Page is used to create templates. The Master Page is not an actual page of the publication; it is simply used to make sure that the pages in the publication are consistent. The settings made on the Master Page will be applied to all the pages in the publication. It is possible to set the page layout on individual page(s) in a publication, however, you are advised to set up a Master Page.

▶▶ How to... *display the Master Page*

1 Click on the **View** menu.

2 Click on **Master Page**.

3 The **Master Page** will be displayed and the **Edit Master Pages** toolbar will be displayed somewhere on the page (Figure 4.3).

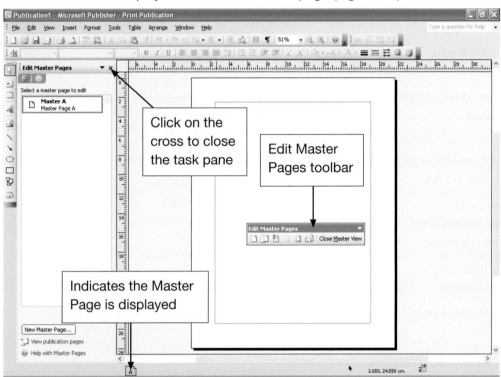

Click on the cross to close the task pane

Edit Master Pages toolbar

Indicates the Master Page is displayed

TIP!

If you close a file while in Master Page view, it may not reopen in Master Page view. To work in Master Page view, you must remember to display the Master Page again.

FIGURE 4.3 Displaying the Master Page

4 The Page Navigation button to the left of the status bar displays as A when the Master Page is displayed.

5 To keep your screen clear, click on the cross to close the **Edit Master Pages** task pane.

Display the Master Page

1 In your **Publication1**, display the Master Page.

2 Locate the Page Navigation button.

3 Locate the Edit Master Pages toolbar.

4 Close the Edit Master Pages task pane.

5 Keep the Master Page open.

Orientation

Orientation is the direction in which a page of a publication will be displayed. *Portrait* orientation will have the short edge of the paper at the top of the page and is referred to in desktop publishing as *tall*. *Landscape* orientation will have the long edge of the paper at the top of the page and is referred to as *wide*.

▶▶ How to... set the page size and orientation

1 Click on the **File** menu.

2 Click on **Page Setup**.

3 The **Page Setup** dialogue box will be displayed (Figure 4.4).

4 Click on the **Printer and Paper** tab.

5 Click on the drop-down arrow to the right of **Size**.

6 A list of available sizes will be displayed. Scroll up to the top of the list and click on **A4**.

7 Orientation can be set by selecting the **Layout** tab or the **Printer and Paper** tab.

8 Click on the button for **Portrait** or **Landscape**.

9 Observe how the **Preview** on the right changes as you select options.

10 Click on **OK**.

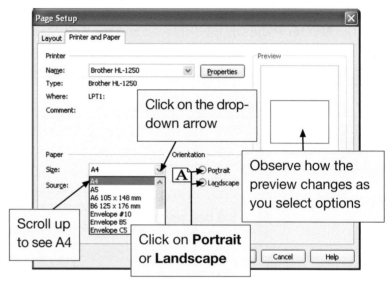

FIGURE 4.4 The Page Setup dialogue box

▶▶ How to... save a publication

1 Click on the **File** menu.

2 Click on **Save As**.

3 The **Save As** dialogue box will be displayed (Figure 4.5).

4 Click on the drop-down arrow to the right of the **Save in** box.

5 A list of user areas will be displayed.

6 Double-click on the folder(s) in your user area to open your working folder.

7 In the **File name** box, delete any existing text.

FIGURE 4.5 The Save As dialogue box

TIP!

To save into a new folder, click on the **Create New Folder**  icon, enter the folder name, click **OK**.

8 Enter the required filename.

9 In the **Save as type** box, make sure **Publisher Files** is displayed.

10 Click on **Save**.

Check your understanding **Set the page size and orientation**

1 In the Master Page of your publication, set the page size to **A4**.

2 Set the page orientation to **Landscape**.

3 Save the publication using the filename **workex1**

What does it mean?

Margins

Margins are the amount of white space (i.e. blank areas on the page) from the edge of the page to the start of the text on the page. In Publisher 2003 the margins are displayed as a blue border on the screen. These margin guides do not display on the printout.

▶▶ **How to...** *set the margins*

1 Click on the **Arrange** menu.

2 Click on **Layout Guides**.

3 The **Layout Guides** dialogue box will be displayed (Figure 4.6).

4 Click in the box for **Left**, delete the existing text and enter the required left margin measurement. You can use the up/down arrows (however, this goes up/down in preset numbers).

5 Click in the boxes for **Right**, **Top** and **Bottom** and set the margins in the same way.

6 Click on **OK**.

TIP!

To move quickly from one margin box to the next, press the **Tab** key.

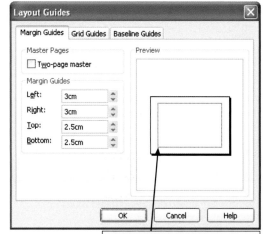

Observe how the position of the blue margin guides changes as you set the margins

FIGURE 4.6 The Layout Guides dialogue box

Check your understanding **Set the margins**

1 In the Master Page of your publication **workex1**, set the margins as follows:

Left	**3cm**
Right	**3cm**
Top	**2.5cm**
Bottom	**2.5cm**

2 Save the publication keeping the filename **workex1**.

Headers and footers

A header is the space within the top margin, and a footer is the space within the bottom margin. Headers and footers are common identifiers at the top and bottom of a page. Special features such as a name, the date and page numbers can be inserted into a header or footer.

▶▶ How to... *insert headers and footers*

1 Click on the **View** menu.

2 Click on **Header and Footer**.

3 The **Header** section of the publication will be displayed in the margin area at the top of the page in a text box (dashed line frame with round handles) (Figure 4.7).

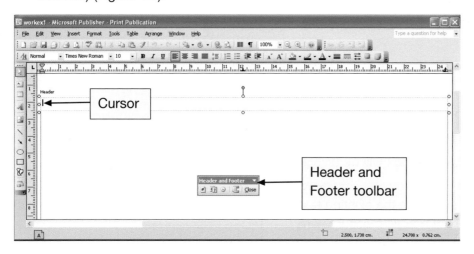

FIGURE 4.7 Inserting headers and footers

4 The **Header and Footer** toolbar will be displayed somewhere on the screen and the cursor will usually be flashing in the left section of the header.

5 Enter any required text (e.g. your name) in the header and/or click on the **Show Header/Footer** 🔲 icon on the **Header and Footer** toolbar to switch to the footer.

6 Enter the required text in the footer.

Note: header/footer text can be entered in any position and in any font type and size within the text box.

7 Click on the Close button on the **Header and Footer** toolbar.

After you have inserted headers or footers, the blue margin guide at the top and bottom of the page will not be displayed. Instead, the header and footer text boxes will be displayed (see Figure 4.8).

▶▶ How to... *close a publication*

1   Click on the **File** menu.

2   Click on **Close**.

▶▶ How to... *open a publication*

Method 1 – open a publication from within Publisher:

1   Click on the **File** menu.

2   Click on **Open** *or* click on the **Open** 📂 icon.

3   The **Open Publication** dialogue box will be displayed.

4   Click on the drop-down arrow to the right of the **Look in** box. A list of user areas is displayed.

5   Open the folders (and sub-folders) in your user area containing the publication.

6   In the **Files of type** box, make sure that **All Publisher Files** is displayed.

7   In the main window, click on the required filename.

8   Click on **Open**.

Method 2 – open a publication from your user area:

1   On the Desktop, double-click on the **My Computer** icon.

2   The **My Computer** window will open.

3   Double-click to open the folders (and subfolders) in your user area containing the publication.

4   The files in the folder will be displayed.

5   Double-click on the publication file.

6   The file will open in Publisher.

Using the Zoom tools

After you have inserted headers or footers, or when you are working on a publication, you may want to change how you view the page on the screen.

1   To view the whole page, click on the drop-down arrow next to the **Zoom** box and click on **Whole Page** or **Page Width** (Figure 4.11).

2   To zoom in to a selected area (e.g. a header/footer, a text box or an image), select the text box or image, click on the drop-down arrow next to the **Zoom** box and click on **Selected Objects** *or* click on the **Zoom In** 🔍 and **Zoom Out** 🔍 icons on the toolbar.

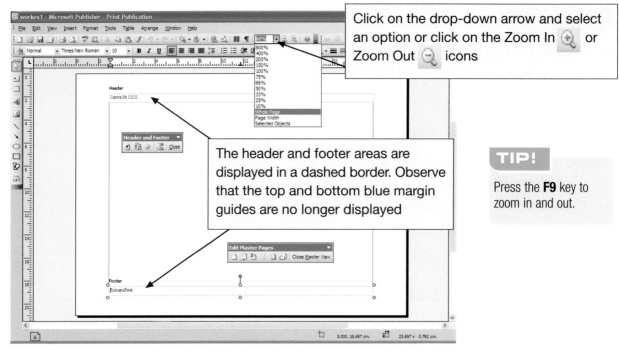

Click on the drop-down arrow and select an option or click on the Zoom In 🔍 or Zoom Out 🔍 icons

The header and footer areas are displayed in a dashed border. Observe that the top and bottom blue margin guides are no longer displayed

TIP!

Press the **F9** key to zoom in and out.

FIGURE 4.8 Using the Zoom tools

Check your understanding *Insert headers and footers*

1   In the Master Page of your publication **workex1**, insert the following headers and footers. You may use any alignment, font type and font size.

   Header your **centre number**
   Footer   your **first** and **last name**

2   Save the publication keeping the filename **workex1**.

3   Practise using the zoom tools:

   ○ zoom into the header
   ○ zoom into the footer
   ○ view the whole page
   ○ zoom to 50%
   ○ display the page width.

Understanding publication page layout

You will normally need to create a publication with a page-wide heading above two or three equally sized columns of text in portrait or landscape orientation. You will need to set the space between columns to a specified measurement.

Look at the example page layouts shown in Figures 4.9 and 4.10.

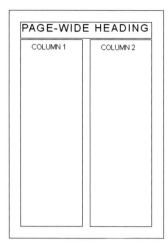

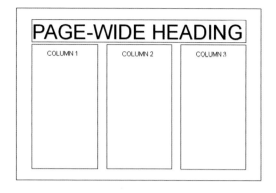

FIGURE 4.9 Publication in portrait orientation with two equal columns of text

FIGURE 4.10 Publication in landscape orientation with three equal columns of text

The page layout can be set up as follows:

1   Create individual text boxes for each column using column guides or ruler guides.

2   Create one text box for all the columns. Set the text box properties to display the required number of columns and the space between columns.

Using column guides allows you to have complete control over the text flow (where the text will be positioned in each column). This is useful if you want to create a leaflet that will be folded in two or three or is going to be printed double-sided.

Creating one text box is a quicker and simpler method of setting the page layout. The inserted text will always start at the top of column 1 (unless you place an image above the text in column 1). This is the method you will learn for Level 1.

The Text Box tool

In Publisher, text can only be entered or inserted from another file into a text box, it cannot be entered or inserted directly into a publication page. You will need to create one text box for the heading and another text box for the columns of text (the body text).

Before you create a text box:

1   Make sure that you have set the page margins correctly as you will be aligning the text box to the margins.

2   Close **Master Page** view: click on the **View** menu, click on **Master Page** or click the Close Master View button on the **Edit Master Pages** toolbar.

3 Check that the **Page Navigation** displays the page number 1 in the Status bar.

4 Make sure the whole page is displayed on screen. Adjust the zoom if required.

▶▶ How to... _create a text box for the heading_

You will be creating a rectangle beginning at the top left corner of the page, below the Header text box, beginning at the left margin guide and drawing diagonally across the page up to the right margin guide. The height of the text box is judged by the eye and can be increased or reduced after it is drawn.

1 Click on the **Text Box** icon [A] on the **Objects** toolbar.

2 Move the mouse into the page. The mouse pointer changes to a cross **+**.

3 Position the mouse at the top left corner within the page, immediately below the Header text box and on the blue left margin guide.

4 Click and drag the mouse to draw a rectangle across the page up to the blue right-hand margin guide.

5 Release the mouse button.

6 The text box will be displayed on the page with round handles around it (Figure 4.11).

7 Zoom in to the page to check that the text box is lined up correctly with the left and right margins and with the Header text box.

Once you have created the box you can change the height, width or position of it.

TIP!

The **Objects** toolbar is usually displayed on the left of the screen.

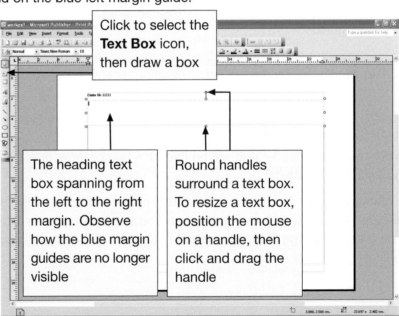

Click to select the **Text Box** icon, then draw a box

The heading text box spanning from the left to the right margin. Observe how the blue margin guides are no longer visible

Round handles surround a text box. To resize a text box, position the mouse on a handle, then click and drag the handle

FIGURE 4.11 Creating a text box for the heading

What does it mean?

Frame
A frame is another word for a text box.

▶▶ How to... _adjust the height or width of a text box_

Before you begin, make sure the text box is selected (round handles displayed). To select a text box click once in it.

1   To adjust the height of a text box, position the mouse pointer on a round handle at the bottom or top of the box. The mouse pointer changes to a double-ended arrow $\updownarrow$. Drag the handle in the direction required (up or down) (Figure 4.12).

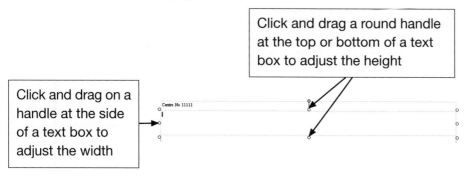

Click and drag a round handle at the top or bottom of a text box to adjust the height

Click and drag on a handle at the side of a text box to adjust the width

FIGURE 4.12 Adjusting the height or width of a text box

2   To adjust the width of a text box, position the mouse pointer on a round handle at the left or right of a box. The mouse pointer changes to a double-ended arrow $\leftrightarrow$. Drag the handle in the direction required.

Create a page-wide heading text box

1   In your publication **workex1**, make sure that you are not in **Master Page** view.

2   Create a text box for the heading at the top of the page.

3   Make sure the text box extends across the width of the page from the left to the right margin, and that the top of the box is positioned at the very top of the page immediately below the Header text box.

4   Check that the height of the box is appropriate for a heading.

5   Adjust the height and/or width of the text box if required. However, this text box can also be adjusted after the heading text has been entered and formatted.

6   Save the publication keeping the filename **workex1**.

Understanding text box properties

The default setting for text boxes in Publisher 2003 is for the top, bottom, left and right margins set to 0.1016 cm. These margin settings within the text box do *not* display on screen (unlike the blue page margin guides). If you do not change the default text box margin settings your text will not extend to the edges of the text box correctly. On a printout, the actual page margins will measure incorrectly because the text is set further in to the text box. You *must* change the Publisher default setting so that the text box margins are set to zero for the heading and the main text box.

1   Make sure the text box is selected (round handles displayed).

2   Click on the **Format** menu.

3   Click on **Text Box**.

4   The **Format Text Box** dialogue box will be displayed (Figure 4.13).

5   Click on the **Text Box** tab.

6   Click on the drop-down arrow to set the **Left** margin to **0** (or click in the **Left** box and enter **0**).

7   Set the **Top, Right** and **Bottom** margins to **0 cm**.

8   Click on the **Colors and Lines** tab.

9   Click to place a tick in the box for **Apply settings to new text boxes** (Figure 4.14). This will ensure that the text box margins will be set to zero for any other text boxes that you create in this publication.

10 Click on **OK**.

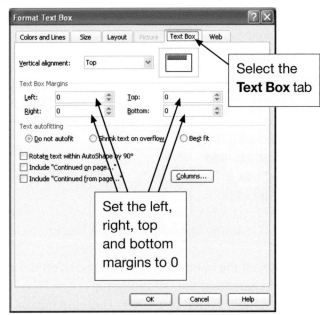

FIGURE 4.13 The Format Text Box dialogue box

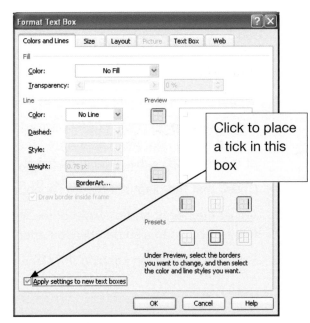

FIGURE 4.14 Apply settings to new text boxes

Check your understanding **Set the text box margins to zero**

1   In your publication **workex1**, make sure the heading text box is selected (round handles displayed).

2   Set the top, bottom, left and right margins to **0 cm**.

3   Save the publication keeping the filename **workex1**.

1 Click in the text box. A cursor will be displayed.

2 On the **Formatting** toolbar, check the font size displayed in the **Font Size** box. If it is small (10 to 14), it will be difficult to see the text being entered.

3 Click on the drop-down arrow next to the **Font Size** `10 ▼` box and select a larger font size (22 to 28) for the time being. You will change the font size again later.

4 Enter the required heading.

TIP!

If the text size is small, a message in a yellow callout box (a tippage) may be displayed. Publisher displays these tippages as helpful hints.

Check your understanding **Enter the heading**

1 In your publication **workex1**, enter the heading **WORK EXPERIENCE** in the heading text box.

2 The heading may be in any font type for the time being.

3 Save the publication keeping the filename **workex1**.

TIP!

Remember to enter text in the same case as shown.

Highlighting text

To format text you will need to highlight (select) the text first (see table below).

TEXT	HOW TO HIGHLIGHT
A word	Position the mouse pointer over the word and **double-click**
A heading or subheading	Position the mouse pointer just before the first word (of the heading/subheading) and click. Hold down the **Shift** key, position the mouse pointer just after the last word (of the heading/subheading) and click
A paragraph	Position the mouse pointer anywhere in the paragraph and triple-click (click three times very quickly)
All the text in a text box	Press the **Ctrl** and **A** keys at the same time

Methods of highlighting text in a publication

Serif and sans serif font types

There are two categories of font that you will need to use and distinguish between: serif and sans serif.

It is important to understand that serif and sans serif are not font names. So, if you look for serif or sans serif in the list of available fonts in Publisher, you will not be able to find it. Serif and sans serif are font categories, not font names.

A serif font has serifs (small strokes) at the edge of each letter.

Look at this letter . The circled parts of the letter T are the serifs.

A sans serif font has no extremities. Look at this letter . It has no serifs (no strokes at the end of the characters).

There are many different font typefaces/designs in the serif and sans serif categories (see table opposite).

When instructed to use a sans serif font, you may select any font from the sans serif font category. Similarly, when instructed to use a serif font, you may select any font from the serif font category.

SERIF FONTS	SANS SERIF FONTS
Times New Roman	Arial
Garamond	Verdana
Palatino	Comic Sans MS
Photina MT	Tahoma
Bodoni MT	Gill Sans MT

Examples of serif and sans serif fonts

▶▶ How to... *select a font*

1 Highlight the required text.

2 On the **Formatting** toolbar, click on the drop-down arrow to the right of the **Font** box.

3 A list of available fonts will be displayed (Figure 4.15).

4 If the required font is displayed, click on the font or scroll down to select other fonts, or enter the first few letters of a font name in the **Font** box.

5 The font of the selected text will change.

6 Click in a blank area to deselect the text (remove the highlight).

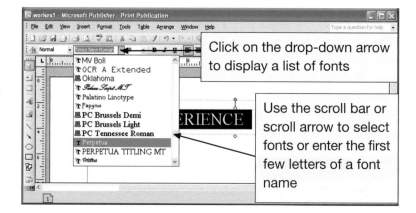

Click on the drop-down arrow to display a list of fonts

Use the scroll bar or scroll arrow to select fonts or enter the first few letters of a font name

FIGURE 4.15 Selecting a font

Check your understanding *Format the heading font*

1 In your publication **workex1**, highlight the heading and select a serif font.

2 Highlight the heading and select a different serif font (experiment with serif font types).

3 Format the heading **WORK EXPERIENCE** in any serif font (e.g. Times New Roman).

4 Save the publication keeping the filename **workex1**.

Formatting text to fit in a text box

There are a number of formatting techniques that can be used to fit text within a text box. These include the following:

1   Using **Best fit**: applies to heading text.

2   Formatting the **font size**: applies to heading and body text.

3   Amending the **kerning**: applies to heading and body text.

4   Amending the **leading**: applies to body text.

Best fit is a quick way of fitting the heading text, however, this option does not always extend the text to span the full width of the text box; it may depend on the height of the text box. Therefore, you will learn how to change the font size and kerning in order to fit the heading text more precisely.

Formatting the font size

There are various methods of changing the font size. For example:

1   On the **Formatting** toolbar, click on the drop-down arrow to the right of the **Font Size** box and select a size *or* enter a custom size, including a number after the decimal point.

2   Click on the **Increase Font Size** A˄ or **Decrease Font Size** A˅ icons.

3   Through the **Format** menu.

4   Using the keyboard.

Observing the change in font size and kerning on screen

You will learn how to format the font size and character spacing by increasing or decreasing the size and the spacing by one point at a time using the keyboard and, as you do, you will see each change on the screen in the text box. This way you will be able to set the text to fit within a text box more precisely.

▶▶ How to... *format the font size*

1   Highlight the relevant text.

2   To *increase* the font size hold down the **Ctrl** key on the keyboard and tap the **closing** square bracket key **]**. The text will increase by one point each time you tap the square bracket.

3   When the size displayed fits most of the width of the text box (before a word becomes hyphenated!), release the **Ctrl** and **square bracket** keys.

What does it mean?

Kerning
Kerning is the space between each character (letter).

What does it mean?

Leading
(pronounced ledding) is another term for line spacing – the space between the lines of text.

What does it mean?

Point
Point is a unit of measurement of font size – 1 point equals 1/72 inch.

TIP!

As you increase the heading text size, the height of the letters will increase. You may notice that not all the text is visible in the text box. Do not be concerned as the height of the text box can be adjusted later.

4   At this point there may be some white space on the right-hand side of the text. Do not be concerned – you will learn how to adjust the kerning (character spacing).

5   To *decrease* the text size: hold down the **Ctrl** key and tap the **opening** square bracket **[**. The text will decrease by one point at a time.

▶▶ *How to...*   set the character spacing (kerning)

1   Highlight the relevant text.

2   To *increase* the character spacing: hold down the **Ctrl** and the **Shift** keys and tap the **closing** square bracket key **]**. The space between each letter will increase each time you tap the square bracket.

3   To *decrease* the character spacing: hold down the **Ctrl** and the **Shift** keys and tap the **opening** square bracket **[**. The space between each letter will decrease each time you tap the square bracket.

4   When the text extends across the full width of the text box, release the **Ctrl**, **Shift** and **square bracket** keys.

5   Adjust the height of the text box as needed.

What does it mean?

Hyphenation
A word at the end of a line of text is split (broken) with a hyphen in between. For example:

hyphen-
ation

TIP!

In an OCR assignment, the instruction is that there should be no more than 1cm of white space to the left or right between the heading and the margins. Using this method you can achieve minimal white space on either side.

Check your understanding Format the heading text size and kerning

1   In your publication **workex1**, format the size of the heading **WORK EXPERIENCE** so that the text fills most, but not all, of the space in the text box.

2   Adjust the character spacing (kerning) so that the text extends across the full width of the text box.

3   Make sure there is minimal white space on the left or the right of the heading text within the text box.

4   Ensure that all the text is fully visible in the text box and that all the text is displayed on one line.

5   If text is not fully displayed, increase the bottom height of the text box.

6   If text is displayed in full, check to see if the height of the text box should be reduced. There should not be unnecessary white space at the bottom of the text box below the text. Adjust the bottom height of the text box if required.

7   Save the publication keeping the filename **workex1**.

Creating a text box for the body text

TIP!

In an OCR assignment you will not be instructed to set the text box margins to 0 cm. You are expected to know how to use your software.

The majority of the text within the columns is body text, and there will also be some subheadings.

Before you begin, make sure that:

○ the size and position of the heading text box are absolutely correct – this avoids the need to adjust text boxes after you have inserted text and images; and

○ you are viewing the whole page – adjust the zoom if required.

▶▶ How to... create a text box for the body text

You will be creating a rectangle from the left margin guide beginning immediately below the heading text box and drawing diagonally across the page to the bottom right margin guide to touch the top of the Footer text box.

1 Click on the **Text Box** icon 📇 on the **Objects** toolbar.

2 Move the mouse into the page. The mouse pointer changes to a cross ✛.

3 Position the mouse towards the top left of the page, immediately below the text box that you created for the heading and on the blue left margin guide.

4 Click and drag the mouse to draw a frame diagonally across the page up to the blue right-hand margin guide up to the top edge of the Footer text box.

5 Release the mouse button.

6 The text box will be displayed on the page with round handles surrounding it (Figure 4.16).

7 Zoom in to check the positioning of the text box:

○ The top of the text box should be aligned with the bottom of the heading text box.

○ The two text boxes should not overlap, but the borders of the boxes may touch so that you see only one dashed line.

○ The left and right edges of the text box should be positioned on the blue margin guides so that the blue margin guides are no longer visible.

What does it mean?

Overlap
When the edge of an object is partly positioned over the edge of another object.

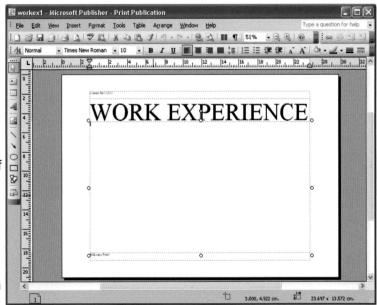

FIGURE 4.16 Creating a text box for the body text

⊙ If your text box extends into the margin area or is not wide enough, the blue left and/or right margin guide will be visible.

8 Click and drag the appropriate round handle to size the text box correctly.

9 Check that the text box margins are set to **0 cm**.

Check your understanding — Create a text box for the body text

1 In your publication **workex1**, create a text box for the body text below the text box for the heading WORK EXPERIENCE.

2 The text box should fill the entire page below the heading to the bottom of the page above the Footer text box.

3 Make sure the text box spans the full width of the page but does not extend into the margin area.

4 You should not see any blue margin guides.

5 Make any necessary adjustments to the size of the text box.

6 Make sure all the text box margins are set to **0 cm**.

7 Save your publication keeping the filename **workex1**.

▶▶ How to... set up columns in a text box

1 Click in the text box to select it (round handles displayed).

2 Click on the **Format** menu.

3 Click on **Text Box**.

4 The **Format Text Box** dialogue box will be displayed.

5 Select the **Text Box** tab.

6 Click on the [Columns...] button in this dialogue box.

7 The **Columns** dialogue box will be displayed (Figure 4.17).

8 Use the up arrow to select the number of columns (or click in the box and enter a number, if you do, the **Spacing** box will remain greyed out).

9 Use the up/down arrow to select the required spacing between columns (or click in the box and enter the measurement – there is no need to enter **cm** as Publisher will insert this).

10 Observe how the Preview on the right changes as you select options.

11 Click on **OK**.

12 The **Format Text Box** dialogue box will be displayed.

13 Click on **OK** to close this dialogue box.

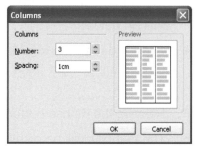

FIGURE 4.17 The Columns dialogue box

TIP!

If you open the **Columns** dialogue box again after you have set the spacing, you will see that Publisher changes the figure for the spacing fractionally (e.g. **1cm**, displays as **0.998cm**). This is acceptable.

TIP!

Publisher will automatically set the columns to be of equal width – you do not need to select any options for equal column width.

Displaying column guides

It is useful to display column guides to help you align objects (e.g. images within a column). The column guides only display on the screen; they do not display on printouts (Publisher 2003 only).

▶▶ How to... *display the column guides*

1   Click in a text box to select it (round handles will be displayed).

2   Click on the **Arrange** menu.

3   Click on **Layout Guides**.

4   The **Layout Guides** dialogue box will be displayed (Figure 4.18).

5   Select the **Grid Guides** tab.

6   In the **Columns** box, enter the number of columns in your publication (or use the up/down arrows).

7   In the **Spacing** box, enter the spacing between the columns that you set for the publication.

8   Click on **OK**.

9   Blue column guides will be displayed on the screen to show the width of each column and the space between columns.

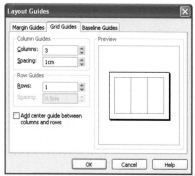

FIGURE 4.18 The Layout Guides dialogue box

Check your understanding *Set up the number of columns, the space between columns and display column guides*

1   In your publication **workex1**, in the text box you created for the body text, create **three** equal columns.

2   Set the space between columns to be **1cm**

3   Display column guides for the three columns, and set the spacing to **1cm**

4   Save the publication keeping the filename **workex1**

By working through Section 1 you will have learnt the skills listed below. Read each item to help you decide how confident you feel about each skill.

- start Publisher and understand the Publisher window
- understand and use the Master Page
- set the page size and orientation
- save a publication
- set the margins
- insert headers and footers
- close a publication
- open a publication (from within Publisher and from My Computer)
- understand the publication page layout
- understand and create text boxes
- use the zoom tools
- adjust the height or width of a text box
- set the text box margins
- enter a heading
- highlight text
- differentiate between serif and sans serif fonts
- format the font
- format the font size
- set the character spacing (kerning)
- set up columns in a text box
- display column guides.

If you think you need more practice on any of the skills above, go back and work through the skill(s) again.

If you feel confident, move on to Section 2.

LEARNING OUTCOMES

In this section you will learn how to:

- import (insert) a text file
- check that all the text in the text file has been inserted:
  - minimize Publisher
  - open a text file
  - print a text file
  - close a text file
  - maximize Publisher
- switch off hyphenation
- align text
- check the spelling
- import (insert) images
- set the text flow for images or shapes
- print a composite copy
- exit Publisher.

Working with a provided text file

In a publication, text can be entered in a text box or, if text has already been prepared in another file, it can be inserted easily into a text box. You will learn how to insert prepared text from a provided text file for the main part of the publication (body text).

The text file must be inserted into the publication after the text box has been set up correctly (i.e. it is in the correct position, the margins have been set to 0 cm, the number of columns and the space between columns have been set up).

> **▶▶ How to...** *import (insert) a text file*

1 Click in the text box in which the text is to be inserted (round handles are displayed and a cursor will flash in the top left corner).

2 Click on the **Insert** menu.

3 Click on **Text File**.

What does it mean?

Text file
A file containing plain text that is not formatted. A text file can be read on most computers – it is referred to as a generic file. A text file has a **.txt** file extension.

What does it mean?

File extension
A dot and 3 or 4 letters after a filename which shows the file type.

4 The **Insert Text** dialogue box will be displayed (Figure 4.19).

5 Click on the drop-down arrow to the right of the **Look in** box.

6 A list of user areas will be displayed.

7 Locate your user area and the folder (and subfolders) in your user area where the file is saved.

8 In the **Files of type** box, check that **All Text Formats** is displayed.

9 In the main window, click on the file to be inserted. The filename will be highlighted (usually in blue).

10 Click on **OK**.

11 The **File Conversion** dialogue box *may* be displayed (Figure 4.20). If it does, check the button for **Windows (Default)** is selected, then click on **OK**.

12 The text file will be inserted into the publication (Figure 4.21).

13 Use the **Zoom In** and **Zoom Out** tools on the **Standard** toolbar to zoom in to the publication.

14 Save the publication.

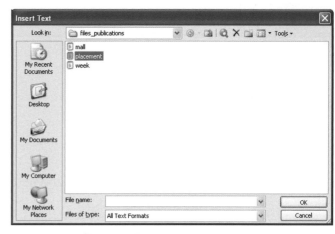

FIGURE 4.19 The Insert Text dialogue box

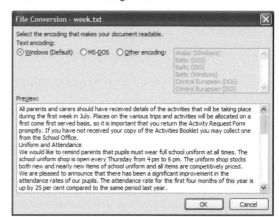

FIGURE 4.20 The File Conversion dialogue box

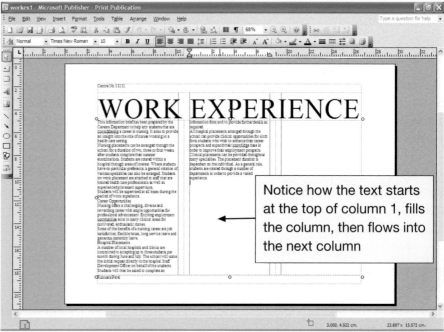

Notice how the text starts at the top of column 1, fills the column, then flows into the next column

FIGURE 4.21 The text file inserted into the publication

For this task you will need the file **placement** from the folder **files_publications**.

1 In your publication **workex1**, insert the text file **placement** into the main text box.

2 The text should begin at the top of column 1 below the heading. It should fill the first column then flow under the heading into the second column.

3 Zoom in to the publication to see the text more clearly.

4 Save the publication keeping the filename **workex1**.

Checking that all text is imported and remains visible on the page

When a text file is inserted into Publisher, all the text will normally be inserted correctly if the columns are set up correctly. However, if you make amendments to the publication or to the default font size, it is possible that some of the text, particularly at the end of the publication, may not fit on the page and will therefore not display.

One sure way of checking that all the original text from the text file has been imported correctly and remains displayed when you make amendments is to open and print the original text file.

TIP!

Import a text file is also referred to as *insert a text file*. In Publisher, the option that you will select from the menu is **Insert**.

▶▶ How to... *minimize Publisher*

1 Before you begin, make sure you have saved the publication.

2 Click on the **Minimize** icon [_] at the top right of the screen.

▶▶ How to... *open the text file*

1 On the **Desktop**, double-click on the **My Computer** icon.

2 The **My Computer** window will be displayed.

3 Double-click to open your user area then double-click to open the folders (and subfolders) in your user area containing the text file (Figure 4.22).

4 Double-click on the required text file icon [icon].

5 The file will open in **Notepad**.

It is difficult to read all the text in Notepad as it is not a WYSIWYG editor, so you are advised to print the file.

FIGURE 4.22 Locating the text file

What does it mean?

WYSIWYG
What You See Is What You Get. A file on screen is how it will display when printed.

▶▶ **How to...** *print the text file*

1   Click on the **File** menu.

2   Click on **Print**.

3   The **Print** dialogue box will be displayed.

4   Click on the **Print** button.

Using the printout you can check that all the text remains displayed on the original and on the amended publication.

▶▶ **How to...** *close the text file*

1   Click on the **File** menu.

2   Click on **Exit**.

▶▶ **How to...** *maximize Publisher*

1   On the taskbar (at the bottom of the screen), click once on the minimized Publisher icon to maximize your publication (Figure 4.23).

Click once on the Publisher icon

FIGURE 4.23 Maximizing Publisher

2   Use the **Zoom** tools to zoom in to various parts of the publication, particularly the last paragraph, to make sure that all the text is fully displayed on the page.

Check your understanding *Open and print a text file*

Before you begin, if your publication is open, make sure you have saved it, then minimize Publisher.

1   From the Desktop, open your user area, and open the folder(s) in your user area to locate the files for the publication.

2   Open the text file **placement**.

3   Print this file.

4   Close the text file.

5   Maximize your publication, zoom in to the page and check that all the text has been inserted correctly by comparing the text in the publication to the printed text file. In particular, check the last few lines.

6   Keep a copy of the printed text file (when you have amended the publication, you will need to check that all the text remains displayed on the page).

The default setting in Publisher is to hyphenate words (split a word over two lines). You are advised to change this setting as it is considered to be good practice not to split whole words and it is easier to read text where words are not 'broken'. A phrase such as double-click or life-size should always be hyphenated.

1 Click in the text box in which you want to switch hyphenation off (normally the main text box for the body text).

2 Click on the **Tools** menu.

3 Click on **Language**, then click on **Hyphenation**.

4 The **Hyphenation** dialogue box will be displayed (Figure 4.24).

5 Click to remove the tick in the box for **Automatically hyphenate this story**.

6 Click on **OK**.

What does it mean?

Story
Related text, often from an imported text file, that flows into a text box and/or columns.

FIGURE 4.24 The Hyphenation dialogue box

Check your understanding — Switch hyphenation off

1 In your publication **workex1**, click in the main text box for the body text.

2 Switch hyphenation off.

3 Save the publication keeping the same filename.

Formatting text

Formatting text means changing the appearance of text. Serif and sans serif fonts, formatting the text size and setting the character spacing were covered in Section 1.

Text alignment

Alignment in a publication is how the text lines up with the left and right sides of the column (or of a text box). Within a column or text box, text can be aligned to the *left*, *centre*, *right*; or to the left and right, referred to as *justified* text. Right-aligned text is not frequently used in single-page publications.

Left-aligned text has a neat left-hand edge and a ragged right-hand edge as displayed in the text you are reading.

Justified text (sometimes referred to as fully justified) has straight edges on both sides. Wider spaces appear between words.

Centred text is used for headings and subheadings in publications. The text is positioned centrally in a column or in a text frame.

See Section 1 for methods of highlighting:

1   Highlight the relevant text.

2   To *left-align* text, click on the **Align Left** ☰ icon.

3   To *fully justify* text, click on the **Justify** ☰ icon.

4   To *centre* text, click the **Center** ☰ icon.

Check your understanding Format the imported text

1   In your publication **workex1**, format the imported body text to:

left-aligned
any **serif** font (e.g. Times New Roman).

2   Save your publication keeping the filename **workex1**.

▶▶ **How to...** *check the spelling*

1   Click on the **Spelling and Grammar** ✔ icon.

2   Publisher will check the publication for spelling errors.

3   If the spell checker finds an error, the **Check Spelling** dialogue box will be displayed (Figure 4.25).

4   The incorrect word is displayed in the **Not in dictionary** box.

5   Alternative spellings may display in the **Change to** box (as the errors in the text file are deliberate there will usually be a suggestion).

6   Click on the **Change** button.

7   If the word is spelt correctly (e.g. the name of a person or place), click on **Ignore**.

8   The dialogue box shown in Figure 4.26 may be displayed. Click on **Yes**.

9   Publisher will continue the spell check. When the spell check is complete, a dialogue box will be displayed (Figure 4.27).

10   Click on **OK**.

> **TIP!**
>
> There will be approximately three deliberate spelling errors in the text file.

FIGURE 4.25 The Check Spelling dialogue box

FIGURE 4.26 Continuing spell check

FIGURE 4.27 Spell check completed

1 In your publication **workex1**, carry out a spell check.

2 Correct the three spelling errors.

3 Do not make any other amendments to the text file.

4 Save the publication keeping the filename **workex1**.

Importing images

There are a number of ways of inserting images into a publication:

1 Select the **Picture Frame** tool, select the option to insert a **Picture from File** and create the frame in the required position.

2 Insert an image directly into the publication without creating a picture frame: click on the **Insert** menu, click on **Picture**, click on **File**, locate the picture, click on **Insert**, then resize and move the image.

3 Select the **Picture Frame** tool and create an empty picture frame in the required position, then insert the image into the frame.

Using method 1 ensures that the image is imported into the correct column, in the required position and in an appropriate size. Method 2 is frequently used, but the image may be displayed in the wrong column even though the cursor may have been positioned correctly and may need to be resized. We will use method 1.

▶▶ How to... *import (insert) an image*

1 Click to select the **Picture Frame** icon on the **Objects** toolbar.

2 A menu will be displayed (Figure 4.28).

3 Click on **Picture from File**.

4 The mouse pointer changes to a cross +.

5 Move the mouse pointer into the publication, to the position where you want to insert the

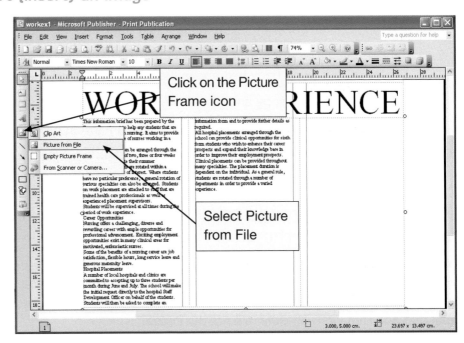

FIGURE 4.28 Importing (inserting) an image

picture. There may be text in this position – do not be concerned, the text will move further down when you draw a frame.

You will draw a box to fit within the column space: not too narrow and not too wide.

6 Click and drag the left mouse button to draw a frame where the image is to be inserted.

7 Release the mouse button.

8 The **Insert Picture** dialogue box will be displayed immediately (Figure 4.29).

9 Click on the drop-down arrow to the right of the **Look in** box.

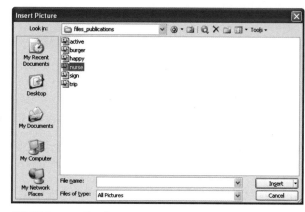

FIGURE 4.29 The Insert Picture dialogue box

10 Double-click to open the folder in your user area containing the image.

11 In the **Files of type** box, make sure that **All Pictures** is displayed.

12 In the main window, click on the image to be inserted.

13 Click on **Insert**.

14 The image will be inserted into the picture frame in your publication.

At this point the size and positioning of the image may not be perfect and there may be text on one or both sides of the image. In this section, you will learn how to format the text wrap for images. In Section 3, you will learn how to resize and move images.

Import images

In your publication **workex1**, you need to insert three images.

1 Import the image **nurse** and place it at the top of the first column below the heading. There should be no body text above the image in column one.

2 Import the image **happy** and place it in the middle of the second column.

3 Import the image **sign** and place it at the bottom of the third column.

4 Save the publication keeping the filename **workex1**.

Formatting the image to display text above and below it (setting the text flow)

When an image is imported into a publication, text may display on one or both sides of the image within a column. This is referred to as text wrap. You are advised to change the wrapping style on all images and shapes so that text does not wrap on either side of the image.

What does it mean?

Text wrap
Text wrap is the way text flows around an object in a text box.

1 Right-click within the image.

2 A menu will be displayed.

3 Click on **Format Picture**.

4 The **Format Picture** dialogue box will be displayed (Figure 4.30).

5 Select the **Layout** tab.

6 In the **Wrapping Style** section, click on **Top and bottom**.

7 Click on **OK**.

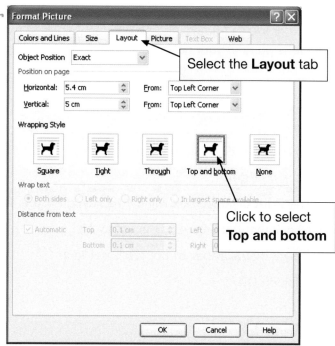

FIGURE 4.30 Setting the text flow

Set the text flow for images

1 In your publication **workex1**, format all three images to set the wrapping style to **Top and bottom**.

2 Make sure that the text does not flow on either side of any of the images.

3 Save your publication keeping the filename **workex1**.

Understanding composite copy

Publications can be printed in different ways. At Level 1, you will not need to be familiar with the different ways – you are simply required to print the entire publication to display all items: text, images, headers/footers and drawing features.

When a publication displays all items on the page, to show how the finished publication will look, it is called a *composite copy*. Printouts need not be in colour, black-and-white prints are perfectly acceptable.

A *composite proof copy* is not the same as a composite copy. On a composite proof copy, if a rough draft of the publication is required to check the layout and positioning of items, you may suppress the printing of pictures so that picture placeholders display instead of the actual images.

Prepare to print a publication

Before you print, click on the **Print Preview** 🔍 icon on the **Standard** toolbar to check your publication.

Your publication will be displayed as it will be printed, with no borders for any text or image frames, and no column guides or margin guides. Click in to various parts of your publication in Print Preview to zoom in. To return to the publication, click | Close .

▶▶ How to... *print a composite copy*

1 Click on the **File** menu.

2 Click on **Print**.

3 The **Print** dialogue box will be displayed (Figure 4.31).

4 Check that the print range is set to **All**.

5 Check that **Number of copies** is set to **1**.

6 Click on **OK**.

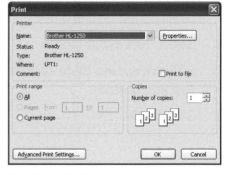

FIGURE 4.31 The Print dialogue box

▶▶ How to... *exit Publisher*

1 Click on the **File** menu.

2 Click on **Exit**.

Print a publication

1 Preview your publication **workex1** and print one copy.

2 Check your printout for accuracy.

3 Close the publication.

4 Exit Publisher.

By working through Section 2 you will have learnt the skills listed below. Read each item to help you decide how confident you feel about each skill.

- ○ import (insert) a text file
- ○ check that all the text in the text file has been inserted:
  - ○ minimize Publisher
  - ○ open a text file
  - ○ print a text file
  - ○ close a text file
  - ○ maximize Publisher
- ○ switch off hyphenation
- ○ align text
- ○ check the spelling
- ○ import (insert) images
- ○ set the text flow for images or shapes
- ○ print a composite copy
- ○ exit Publisher.

If you think you need more practice on any of the skills above, go back and work through the skill(s) again.

If you feel confident, move on to Section 3.

In this section you will learn how to:

- resize an image
- move an image
- flip an image
- crop an image
- draw, format and move a line
- display a border around a text box
- display an outside border around an object
- draw a shape
- set a first-line indent
- set the paragraph spacing
- set the text alignment
- copy and paste text
- find and replace text
- balance columns
- edit text
- format subheadings
- copy formatting.

Manipulating images

When you have inserted images or when you amend a publication, you may want to make some changes to the images (e.g. resize, move, crop, flip). Whenever you work with an image, you must make sure that you keep the original shape of the image. This is referred to as *maintaining the original proportions*. Look at the examples in Figures 4.32–4.34.

FIGURE 4.32 Original image

FIGURE 4.33 Original image resized and original proportions maintained – correct

FIGURE 4.34 Original image resized but now distorted – incorrect

Resizing images

You will normally be required to fit images within the column; they should not extend into the margin or column space. You may need to resize image(s) when you first insert them into a publication or later when you amend a publication.

Resizing images is also useful to help balance columns (balancing columns will be covered later in this section).

▶▶ How to... *resize an image*

Method 1

1 Click once on the image to select it. Round handles will display.

2 Position your mouse on a *corner* handle of the image (see Figure 4.35).

3 The mouse changes to a diagonal arrow ↘ or ↖.

4 Using the left mouse button, click and drag the diagonal arrow inwards to make the image smaller *or* outwards to increase the size of an image.

5 Release the mouse button.

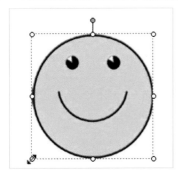

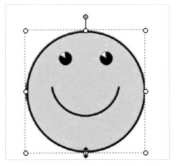

FIGURE 4.35 The correct way to resize using the diagonal arrow at the corner of an image

FIGURE 4.36 The incorrect way to resize using the straight arrow at the side, bottom or top of an image

Method 2

1 Right-click on the picture.

2 A menu will be displayed.

3 Click on **Format Picture**.

4 The **Format Picture** dialogue box will be displayed (Figure 4.37).

5   Select the **Size** tab.

6   Check that there is a tick in the box for **Lock aspect ratio**.

7   *To make the image smaller:* in the **Scale** section, click on the down arrow for **Height**. The width will automatically change.

8   *To make the image bigger:* in the **Scale** section, click on the up arrow for **Height**. The width will automatically change.

9   Click on **OK**.

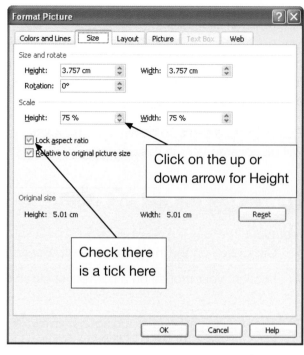

FIGURE 4.37 The Format Picture dialogue box

▶▶ How to... *move images*

1   Position your mouse on the image.

2   The mouse changes to ✛ (a four-headed arrow).

3   Click and drag the image to the required position. Hold down the **Alt** key while dragging the image to give you more precise control.

4   Release the mouse button.

TIP!

If you make a mistake, click on the **Undo** ↺ icon and start again.

TIP!

When moving images, make sure you use the four-headed arrow ✛ , not a double-ended arrow ↕ ↔ or a diagonal arrow ↘ ↗ .

Resize and move images

1   Open your publication **workex1** and save it with the new filename **workex2**

2   Move the image **sign** from the bottom of the third column to the top of the third column.

3   The image should be under the heading text box, and there should be no body text above the image.

4   Reduce the size of the image **happy** in the second column so that it is visibly smaller.

5   Make sure you keep the original proportions of both images.

6   Make sure no images overlap any text or extend into the margin space or space between columns.

7   Save the publication keeping the filename **workex2**.

TIP!

When instructed to increase or reduce the size of an image, it must be visibly bigger or smaller. There is no exact measurement.

1　Click once on an image to select it.

2　Round handles will be displayed around a selected image.

3　Click on the **Arrange** menu.

4　Click on **Rotate or Flip**.

5　Click on **Flip Horizontal** (or **Flip Vertical**).

6　The direction of the image will change – it will be flipped.

What does it mean?

Flip
Flip means to change the direction. An image can be horizontally flipped (the direction is changed from left to right or vice versa) or vertically flipped (it is turned upside down).

Flip image(s)

1　In your publication **workex2**, flip the **nurse** image horizontally.

2　Optional: flip the **happy** image horizontally (the direction of the eyes will change!).

3　Save the publication keeping the filename **workex2**.

Cropping images

To crop an image is to cut out part of it. In Publisher, an image can be cropped from the top, bottom, left or right side or from any of the four corners.

How to... *crop an image*

1　Click once on an image to select it.

2　Round handles will be displayed around a selected image.

3　When an image is selected, the **Picture** toolbar will usually be displayed somewhere on the screen (Figure 4.38). It may be floating (i.e. on the page) or displayed below or to the right of the **Formatting** toolbar.

4　Click on the **Crop** tool ⌗.

5　Thick black lines will be displayed at the top, bottom, left and right edge of the image and at each of the four corners. These are the positions from which the image can be cropped (Figure 4.39).

6　Move the mouse on to the thick border to the position from which you want to crop the image (e.g. to crop from the bottom, move your mouse to the thick black line at the bottom of the image).

Crop tool

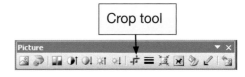

FIGURE 4.38　The Picture toolbar

TIP!

To display the **Picture** toolbar, click on the **View** menu, click on **Toolbars**, then click on **Picture**.

7   Using the left mouse button, click on the thick line and drag it further inwards.

8   Release the mouse button.

9   The image will be cropped.

TIP!

If you make a mistake, click on the **Undo** icon and start again.

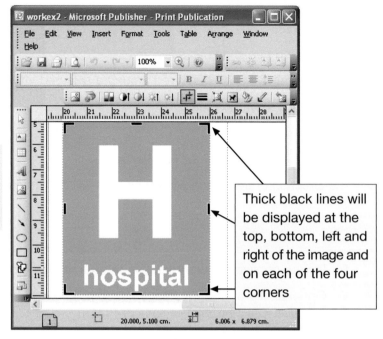

Thick black lines will be displayed at the top, bottom, left and right of the image and on each of the four corners

FIGURE 4.39 The positions from which the image can be cropped

Check your understanding *Crop an image*

1   In your publication **workex2**, crop the image **sign** from the bottom to remove the word **hospital**.

2   Crop the top, left and right sides of the image to remove the excess blue background.

3   Make sure no part of the white **H** in the centre of the image is cropped.

4   After you have cropped the image, make sure the image is positioned at the top of the third column and that there is no body text above the image. Move the image if required.

5   Set the text wrap to top and bottom.

6   Save the publication keeping the filename **workex2**.

TIP!

Zoom into the picture before you begin cropping an image.

Using drawing features

You will need to know how to draw lines, borders and simple shapes. These can be created easily using the **Objects** toolbar, which is usually displayed on the left of the screen.

▶▶ How to... *draw a line*

1   Click on the **Line** ＼ icon on the **Objects** toolbar to select it.

2   Move the mouse to the position where the line should begin.

3   The mouse pointer changes to a cross +.

4   Hold down the left mouse button and click and drag the mouse to draw a line.

5   To draw a straight line, hold down the **Shift** key while drawing the line.

6   When the line is long enough, release the mouse button.

7   Zoom in to the publication to check the positioning of the line. Make sure it does not extend into the margin space.

8   To increase/decrease the line length click on the line to select it. Click and drag one of the ends of the line.

▶▶ How to...   *format the line*

1   Click once on a line to select it.

2   Round handles will be displayed on the left and right ends of the line.

3   On the **Formatting** toolbar, click on the **Line/Border Style** ≡ icon.

4   A drop-down selection of line widths will be displayed (Figure 4.40).

5   Click on an option to select a line thickness, or line style.

TIP!

To change the line to a dotted or dashed line click on the **Dash style** ▦ icon and select an option.

TIP!

pt means point.

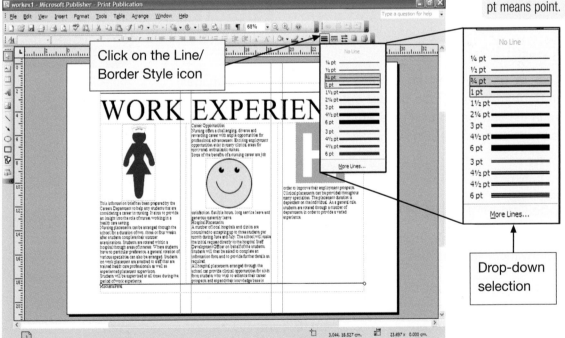

FIGURE 4.40 Formatting a line

If the line is not in the correct position, it can be moved easily:

1 Click once on a line to select it.

2 Round handles will be displayed on both ends.

3 Click and drag with the mouse or tap the cursor (arrow) in the direction you want to move a line.

Draw and format lines

1 In your publication **workex2**, draw a line *above the heading* to separate the bottom of the Header text box and the top of the text box containing the heading WORK EXPERIENCE.

2 The line must extend from the left margin to the right margin. This line will separate the top margin from the top of the publication (i.e. the top of the text box containing the heading).

3 Draw another line *below the body text* to separate the bottom margin area from the text – the line should be drawn at the bottom of the body text box and at the top of the Footer text box.

4 Format both lines to a thickness of **1pt**.

5 Make sure the lines do not extend into the margin area.

6 Save the publication keeping the filename **workex2**.

Understanding borders

Borders can be displayed around existing objects (text boxes, images) using the **Rectangle** tool or the **Border** option; or a box can be drawn anywhere in the publication using the **Rectangle** tool. Alternatively, to display an outside border around an object, it is quicker to use the **Line/Border** icon.

How to... *display a border for a text box*

This method has more border options than the **Line/Border** style icon, e.g. border with/without line between columns, top border etc.

Note: If you display an outside border around a text box, the border will touch the text if the text box margins are set to 0 cm. Therefore, you *must* remember to change the text box margins to, e.g. **0.1 cm**.

1 Click once in a text box to select it.

2 Round handles will be displayed around the object.

3 Right-click in the object.

4 A menu will be displayed.

5 Click on **Format Text Box**.

6 The **Format Text Box** dialogue box will be displayed (Figure 4.41).

7 Select the **Colors and Lines** tab.

8 In the **Presets** section, click on the preview of the type of border required.

9 Click on the drop-down arrow next to **Color** to select a colour, e.g. black.

10 To display a dashed line, click on the drop-down arrow to the right of **Dashed** to select an option.

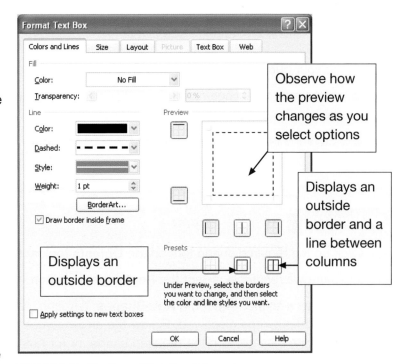

Observe how the preview changes as you select options

Displays an outside border and a line between columns

Displays an outside border

FIGURE 4.41 The Format Text Box dialogue box

11 Click on the drop-down arrow next to **Style** to change the border style.

12 Click on the drop-down arrow next to **Weight** to change the weight.

13 Observe how the preview updates as you select options.

14 Click on **OK**.

▶▶ How to... *display an outside border for an object*

1 Click once on the object (text box/image) to select it. Round handles should display around it.

2 Click on the **Line/Border Style** ☰ or the **Dash Style** ⠿ icon on the **Formatting** toolbar.

3 A selection will be displayed.

4 Click to select a border style.

5 An outside border will be displayed.

6 For text boxes, make sure the border is not touching the text. If it is, format the text box so that the text box margins are *not* 0, e.g. set the margins to 0.1cm.

1 In your publication **workex2**, display a dashed line border around the image **sign**.

2 Make sure the image remains positioned at the top of the column with no body text above it.

3 Save the publication keeping the filename **workex2**.

▶▶ How to... *draw a shape*

1 Click on the required shape tool on the **Objects** toolbar to select it.

   a To draw a *rectangle*, select the **Rectangle** ☐ icon.

   b To draw a *shape*, select the **AutoShapes** 🐭 icon. A list of categories will be displayed. Follow the arrow across the required category, then click on the required shape, or for AutoShapes you may click once to create the shape.

2 The mouse pointer changes to a cross +.

3 Move the mouse to the position where the shape should begin.

4 Hold down the left mouse button and click and drag the mouse to draw the shape.

5 When the shape is drawn to the required size, release the mouse button.

   ○ To resize a shape, refer to **How to... resize an image** on page 37.

   ○ To move a shape, refer to **How to... move images** on page 38.

   ○ To position text above and below a shape, refer to **How to... set the text flow for images and shapes** in Section 2 (page 33).

Text in publications

In desktop publishing, it is conventional to have:

○ one space after a full stop;

○ a first-line indent to identify the beginning of a new paragraph; or

○ one clear line space between paragraphs.

It is good practice not to waste space in publications; too much white space should be avoided where possible.

TIP!

Set the text wrap for drawn shapes (except lines) as follows:

Right-click within the shape, a menu displays, click **Format AutoShape**, a **Format AutoShape** dialogue box displays, select the **Layout** tab, in the **Wrapping Style** section, click on **Top and bottom**, click **OK**.

TIP!

Create a new blank publication and experiment with drawing different shapes, (e.g. a star, a heart shape, a rectangle, arrows, a flag shape and callout boxes).

What does it mean?

First-line indent
First-line indent applies to the body text. The first line of each paragraph is set further in from the left margin (indented) by a small amount so that it is clear where one paragraph starts and the previous one ends.

Setting the paragraph alignment

Setting the paragraph alignment includes setting a first-line indent or a clear line space between paragraphs and setting the text alignment (e.g. left aligned or fully justified).

TIP!

Press **Ctrl** + **A** to highlight all the text in a text box quickly.

▶▶ How to... *set a first-line indent*

1 Click in the main text box and highlight all the text.

2 Click on the **Format** menu.

3 Click on **Paragraph**.

4 The **Paragraph** dialogue box will be displayed.

5 Check that the **Indents and Spacing** tab is selected.

6 In the **Indentation** section, click on the up arrow to the right of **First line** until the required measurement is displayed (Figure 4.42).

7 Click on **OK**.

To set the paragraph spacing and/or text alignment, remain in this dialogue box.

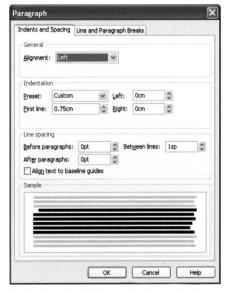

FIGURE 4.42 Setting a first-line indent

TIP!

Select between 0.5 and 1cm for the first-line indent if a measurement is not specified. Alternatively, click on the drop-down arrow to the right of **Preset**, a list will be displayed, select **1st Line Indent**. Publisher will set an indent of 1cm.

▶▶ How to... *set the paragraph spacing*

In a publication, either the first-line indent or the paragraph spacing is set, not both.

1 Click in the main text box and highlight all the text.

2 Click on the **Format** menu.

3 Click on **Paragraph**.

4 The **Paragraph** dialogue box will be displayed.

5 In the **Line spacing** section, click on the up arrow to increase the spacing for **After paragraphs** to about **6pt** (Figure 4.43).

Note: you may select **Before paragraphs** instead, but you should not select both.

6 Click on **OK**.

To set the text alignment, remain in this dialogue box.

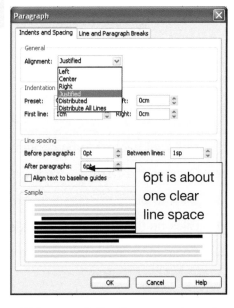

FIGURE 4.43 Setting the paragraph spacing

The text alignment can be set in the **Paragraph** dialogue box or by clicking the relevant alignment icon on the **Formatting** toolbar.

1   Highlight the required text.

2   In the **Paragraph** dialogue box, click on the drop-down arrow to the right of **Alignment** (Figure 4.43).

3   A list will be displayed. Click on the required alignment, OR

Click the relevant alignment icon ≣ ≣ ≣ ≣ on the **Formatting** toolbar.

Check your understanding *Set the paragraph alignment and first-line indent*

1   In your publication **workex2**, highlight all the text in the main text box.

2   Format the text so that each paragraph has a **first-line indent**.

3   Make sure you do *not* insert a clear line space between paragraphs.

4   Format the text to **fully justified**.

5   Format the text to any **sans serif** font (e.g. Arial).

6   Save the publication keeping the filename **workex2**.

Manipulating text

Amending text can include cut (delete), copy and paste, insert, find and replace.

▶▶ **How to...** *copy and paste text*

1   Highlight the text to be copied.

2   Click on the **Copy** 📋 icon on the **Standard** toolbar.

3   Click to place the cursor in the position where the text is to be pasted.

4   Click on the **Paste** 📋 icon on the **Standard** toolbar.

5   Zoom in to check the spacing on either side of the copied text.

▶▶ **How to...** *find and replace text*

1   Click on the **Edit** menu.

2   Click on **Replace**.

3 The **Find and Replace** task pane will be displayed on the left of the screen (Figure 4.44).

4 Check that the **Replace** button is selected.

5 In the **Find what** box, enter the word to be replaced.

6 In the **Replace with** box, enter the new word.

7 Click on the **Replace All** button to replace all instances of the original word.

8 A dialogue box will be displayed informing you that Publisher has finished searching the publication.

9 Click on **OK**.

10 Click on the cross to close the **Find and Replace** task pane.

TIP!

If you click on the **Replace** button – this will replace only one occurrence of the word at a time.

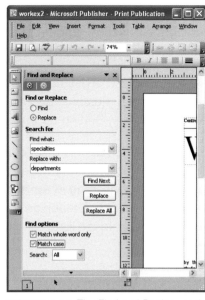

FIGURE 4.44 The Find and Replace task pane

Check your understanding — Find and replace text

1 In your publication **workex2**, find the word **specialties** and replace it with **departments** wherever it occurs in the publication (twice in all).

2 Save the publication keeping the filename **workex2**.

▶▶ How to... *edit text*

1 Zoom into the publication so that you can read the text clearly.

2 Click to place the mouse in the required position.

3 Delete the unwanted text.

4 Enter the required text.

TIP!

Use the **Backspace** key to delete text to the left of the cursor or the **Delete** key to delete text to the right of the cursor.

Manipulating text and images to balance columns

There are a number of techniques that can be used to achieve column balancing:

- resize text.
- amend the character spacing (kerning).
- amend the line spacing (leading).
- resize images and/or shapes.
- change the font type.

TIP!

When balancing columns, the final column does not need to be balanced exactly. There should be no more than two lines of white space (approximately 20mm) at the end of the final column. Less than two lines of white space is acceptable.

Publisher 2003 also has a more advanced feature to balance columns by setting the **baseline guides**. This is covered in the handout on the CD-ROM.

Alternatively, text styles can be set up for the various text areas of a publication (e.g. heading, subheadings, body text). However, at Level 1 this is not necessary. Setting up text styles is covered in the Level 2 book.

To balance columns it is quicker and easier to select all the text (this will include the body text and the subheadings) and format it as required. Then format one subheading in the subheading style and use the Format Painter for the remaining subheadings. To achieve the final column balancing, use any of the techniques listed on page 47 or a combination of more than one technique.

There is no one single option that will achieve perfect column balancing. You will have to make adjustments and see the effect each time.

Amending the text size

When selecting a font size (from the drop-down list on the **Formatting** toolbar or by using **Ctrl** + a **square bracket**), the font sizes change by 1pt. This may not achieve the desired effect (e.g. fitting the text in a text box or column balancing). You can enter a specific font size, including decimals, in the **Font Size** box (e.g. 10.3 on the **Formatting** toolbar). After you have entered the custom number, you *must* press the **Enter** key on the keyboard.

▶▶ How to... *format subheadings*

1 Highlight one subheading.

2 Click on the **Format** menu.

3 Click on **Paragraph**.

4 The **Paragraph** dialogue box will be displayed.

5 Click on the drop-down arrow next to **Preset** and select **Flush Left** (to remove the first-line indent that may have been set for the body text).

6 Click on the drop-down arrow next to **Alignment** and select the required alignment (usually **Left** or **Center** for subheadings).

7 Click on **OK**.

8 The Paragraph dialogue box will close and the subheading will remain highlighted.

9 On the **Formatting** toolbar, click on the drop-down arrow to the right of the **Font** box and select a font type.

10 Select a font size using any of the methods you have learnt.

▶▶ How to... *copy formatting to subheadings*

1 Highlight a subheading that has been formatted as required.

2 Double-click on the **Format Painter** 🖌.

3 Highlight the remaining subheadings.

4 Click on the **Format Painter** again to deselect it or press **Esc**.

▶▶ How to... *copy formatting to paragraphs of text*

This is one way of balancing columns:

1 Format one paragraph (e.g. resize text, amend kerning, amend leading).

2 Highlight the paragraph that has been formatted as required.

3 Double-click on the **Format Painter** .

4 Highlight the remaining paragraphs.

5 Click on the **Format Painter** again to deselect it or press **Esc**.

Note:
If the final column is not balanced to within two line spaces of the previous column, try the following:

○ resize the image(s) and shape(s) maintaining proportions

○ resize the subheadings.

Check your understanding *Edit and format subheadings and body text*

1 In your publication **workex2**, change the body text size to a custom size that includes a decimal, e.g. 10.2.

2 Edit the subheading **Hospital Placements** to be **Clinical Placements**

3 Format this subheading to be larger than the body text and smaller than the heading.

4 Format this subheading to a **sans serif** font style that is different from the body text (e.g. Comic Sans MS).

5 Format this subheading to **left-aligned** (the subheading must not be indented).

6 Copy the formatting for this subheading to the other subheading **Career Opportunities**

7 Save the publication keeping the filename **workex2**.

1   In your publication **workex2**, format the publication so that all columns are balanced at the bottom of the page. You may use any method to achieve this:

   ○   Resize text.

   ○   Resize images (but make sure that, for the images that had to be visibly reduced/enlarged, the change in size is maintained).

   ○   Adjust the kerning (character spacing).

   ○   Adjust the leading (line spacing).

2   Check your final publication:

   ○   Make sure that the heading, subheadings and body text are three different sizes.

   ○   Make sure that all the original text is displayed on one page.

3   Save the publication keeping the filename **workex2**.

4   Use **Print Preview** to check the publication.

5   Print the publication on one page.

6   Close the publication.

7   Exit Publisher.

> **TIP!**
>
> Zoom in to check that all of the imported text remains visible on the page. Refer to your printout of the original text file.

By working through Section 3 you will have learnt the skills listed below. Read each item to help you decide how confident you feel about each skill.

- ○ resize an image
- ○ move an image
- ○ flip an image
- ○ crop an image
- ○ draw, format and move a line
- ○ display a border around a text box
- ○ display an outside border around an object
- ○ draw a shape
- ○ set a first-line indent
- ○ set the paragraph spacing
- ○ set the text alignment
- ○ copy and paste text
- ○ find and replace text
- ○ edit text
- ○ balance columns
- ○ format subheadings
- ○ copy formatting.

If you think you need more practice on any of the skills above, go back and work through the skill(s) again.

If you feel confident, do the Build-up and Practice tasks.

Keep a copy of this page next to you. Refer to it when working through tasks and during assessments.

QUICK REFERENCE – *Create a publication and insert files*

HOW TO...	METHOD
Start Publisher	Click on the Start button → click on All Programs → click on Microsoft Office → click on Microsoft Office Publisher 2003.
Display the Master Page	Click on the View menu → click on Master Page.
Save a publication	Click on the File menu → click on Save As → the Save As dialogue box will be displayed → click on the drop-down arrow next to Save in → a list of user areas will be displayed → double-click on the folder(s) in your user area to open your working folder → in the File name box, delete any existing text → enter the filename → click on Save.
Close a publication	Click on the File menu → click on Close.
Open a publication from within Publisher	Click on the Open icon → the Open Publication dialogue box will be displayed → click on the drop-down arrow next to the Look in box → open the folder in your user area containg the file → in the Files of type box, make sure that All Publisher Files is displayed → click on the required filename → click on Open.
Set the page size and orientation	Click on the File menu → click on Page Setup → the Page Setup dialogue box will be displayed → click on the Printer and Paper tab → click on the drop-down arrow next to Size → scroll up and click on A4 → click on the button for Portrait or Landscape → click on OK.
Set the margins	Click on the Arrange menu → click on Layout Guides → the Layout Guides dialogue box will be displayed → click in the box for Left, delete the existing text and enter the left margin measurement → repeat for the right, top and bottom margins → click on OK.
Insert headers and footers	Click on the View menu → click on Header and Footer → the Header section will be displayed within the margin area → enter any header text → click on the Show Header/Footer icon to switch to the footer → enter the required text → click on Close on the Header and Footer toolbar.
Create a text box for the heading	Click on the Text Box icon from the Objects toolbar → move the mouse into the page, the mouse pointer changes to a cross → position the cross where the text box should begin → click and drag to draw a box up to the blue right-hand margin guide → release the mouse button.

HOW TO...	METHOD
Adjust the height or width of a text frame	Position the mouse pointer on a round handle on one of the sides of the box, the mouse pointer changes to a double-ended arrow ⇗ drag the handle in the direction required.
Set the text box margins	Select the text box ⇗ click on the Format menu ⇗ click on Text Box ⇗ the Format Text Box dialogue box will be displayed ⇗ select the Text Box tab ⇗ set the left, right, top and bottom margins margin to 0 cm ⇗ click on OK.
Enter a heading	Click in the text box ⇗ select a medium font size (e.g. 22 to 28) ⇗ enter the required heading.
Highlight	*A word*: double-click on the word. *A heading or subheading*: position the mouse pointer before the first word and click ⇗ hold down the Shift key ⇗ position the mouse pointer after the last word and click. *A paragraph*: triple-click in the paragraph. *All the text in a text box*: press the Ctrl and A keys.
Format the font	Highlight the required text ⇗ on the Formatting toolbar, click on the drop-down arrow next to the Font box ⇗ a list will be displayed ⇗ click on a font or scroll down to select other fonts and click ⇗ click in a blank area to deselect the text.
Increase font size by one point	Highlight the relevant text ⇗ hold down the Ctrl key and tap the closing square bracket key]
Decrease font size by one point	Highlight the relevant text ⇗ hold down the Ctrl key and tap the opening square bracket [
Increase the character spacing (kerning)	Highlight the relevant text ⇗ hold down the Ctrl and the Shift keys and tap the closing square bracket key]
Decrease the character spacing (kerning)	Highlight the relevant text ⇗ hold down the Ctrl and the Shift keys and tap the opening square bracket [
Create a text box for the body text	Click on the Text Box icon from the Objects toolbar ⇗ move the mouse into the page, the mouse pointer changes to a cross ⇗ position the mouse below the heading text box on the blue left margin guide ⇗ click and drag the mouse diagonally across the page up to the blue right-hand margin guide to the top edge of the Footer frame ⇗ release the mouse button ⇗ set the text box margins to 0 cm.

HOW TO...	METHOD
Set up columns and column spacing in a text box	Click in the text box to select it → click on the Format menu → click on Text Box → the Format Text Box dialogue box will be displayed → select the Text Box tab → click on the Columns button → the Columns dialogue box will be displayed → enter the number of columns → enter the spacing between columns → click on OK → click on OK to close the Format Text Box dialogue box. *Note:* Publisher will automatically set the columns to be of equal width.
Display column guides	Click on the Arrange menu → click on Layout Guides → select the Grid Guides tab → enter the number of columns → enter the spacing between columns → click on OK.
Import (insert) a text file	Click in the text box → click on the Insert menu → click on Text File → the Insert Text dialogue box will be displayed → click on the arrow next to the Look in box → locate the folder where the file is saved → in the Files of type box, check that All Text Formats is displayed → the filename will be highlighted → click on OK → the File Conversion dialogue box *may* be displayed → check Windows (Default) is selected → click on OK.
Check that all the text in the text file has been inserted	*To minimize Publisher:* click on the Minimize icon. *To open the text file:* on the Desktop, double-click on the My Computer icon → the My Computer window will open → double-click to open the folder containing the file → double-click on the required text file → the file will open in Notepad. *To print the text file:* click on the File menu → click on Print → the Print dialogue box will be displayed → click on Print. *To close the text file:* click on the File menu → click on Exit. *To maximize Publisher:* on the taskbar, click once on the Publisher file icon. Use the Zoom tools to zoom into the publication → check to make sure all the text is visible.
Align text	Highlight the relevant text → click on the required alignment icon on the Formatting toolbar.
Check the spelling	Click on the Spelling and Grammar icon → if an error is found, the Check Spelling dialogue box will be displayed → the incorrect word is displayed in the Not in Dictionary box → alternative spellings may display in the Change to box → click on Change → if a word is spelt correctly (e.g. a name), click on Ignore → when the spell check is complete a dialogue box will be displayed → click on OK.

HOW TO...	METHOD
Import (insert) an image	Select the Picture Frame icon from the Objects toolbar → a menu will be displayed → click on Picture from File → the mouse pointer changes to a cross → draw a frame within the column where the image is to be placed → release the mouse button → the Insert Picture dialogue box will be displayed → click on the drop-down arrow next to the Look in box → double-click to open the folder where the image is saved → click on the name of the image to be inserted → click on Insert.
Set the text flow for an image	Right-click within the image → a menu will be displayed → click on Format Picture → the Format Picture dialogue box will be displayed → select the Layout tab → in the Wrapping Style section, click on Top and bottom → click on OK.
Set the text flow for a shape	Right-click within the shape → a menu will be displayed → click on Format AutoShape → the Format AutoShape dialogue box will be displayed → select the Layout tab → in the Wrapping Style section, click on Top and bottom → click on OK.
Switch off hyphenation	Click in the text frame → click on the Tools menu → click on Language → click on Hyphenation → click to remove the tick in the box for Automatically hyphenate this story → click on OK.
Print a composite copy	Click on the File menu → click on Print → the Print dialogue box will be displayed → click on OK.
Exit Publisher	Click on the File menu → click on Exit.

QUICK REFERENCE – Amend a publication

Keep a copy of this page next to you. Refer to it when working through tasks and during assessments.

HOW TO...	METHOD
Resize an image or shape	*Method 1* Click once on an image to select it → position your mouse on a *corner* handle of the image → the pointer changes to a diagonal arrow → click and drag the arrow in the required direction → release the mouse button. *Method 2* Right-click on the picture → a menu will be displayed → click on Format Picture → the Format Picture dialogue box will be displayed → select the Size tab → in the Scaling section, check there is a tick in Lock Aspect Ratio box→ change the Height → click on OK.
Move images or shapes	Position your mouse on the image → the mouse changes to a four-headed arrow → click and drag the image to the required position → release the mouse button.
Flip an image	Select the image → click on the Arrange menu → click on Rotate or Flip → click on Flip Horizontal (or Flip Vertical).
Crop an image	Select the image → from the Picture toolbar, click on the Crop tool → thick black lines will be displayed at the edges → click on a thick black edge and drag the mouse inwards.
Draw a line	Click on the Line icon from the Objects toolbar → the mouse pointer changes to a cross → move the mouse to the position where the line should begin → hold down the left mouse button → click and drag to draw a line → to draw a straight line, hold down the Shift key → release the mouse button.
Format the line	Click once on a line to select it → round handles will be displayed at both ends → on the Formatting toolbar, click on the Line/Border Style icon → a selection will be displayed → click on an option.
Move a line	Click once on a line to select it → round handles will be displayed at both ends → click and drag the mouse or tap the up, down, left or right cursor key.

HOW TO...	METHOD
Display a border for a text box	Click once in a text frame to select it → round handles will be displayed around it → right-click → a menu will be displayed → click on Format Text Box → the Format Text Box dialogue box will be displayed → select the Colors and Lines tab → in the Presets section, click on the preview of the option required. To select a colour, click on the drop-down arrow next to Color → select a colour. To display a dashed line, click the drop-down arrow next to Dashed → select a style. Click on the drop-down arrow next to Style to change the border style → select a style. Click on the drop-down arrow next to Weight to change the weight → select a weight. Click on OK.
Display an outside border around an object	Select the object → round handles will be displayed → on the Formatting toolbar, click on the Line/Border Style or Dash Style icon → a selection will be displayed → select an option. Note: If the outside border is for a text box you may need to change the text box margins.
Draw a shape	Click on the required shape tool from the Objects toolbar → the mouse pointer changes to a cross → move the mouse to the position where the shape should begin → hold down the left mouse button, click and drag the mouse to draw the shape → release the mouse button.
Set a first-line indent	Highlight all the text in a text box → click on the Format menu → click on Paragraph → the Paragraph dialogue box will be displayed → click on the up arrow next to First line to select a measurement or click on the drop-down arrow next to Preset → select 1st Line Indent → click on OK.
Set the paragraph spacing	Highlight all the text → click on the Format menu → click on Paragraph → the Paragraph dialogue box will be displayed → in the Line spacing section, click on the up arrow to increase the spacing for After paragraphs to about 6pt → click on OK.
Set the text alignment	Highlight the relevant text → click on the relevant alignment icon on the Formatting toolbar.
Copy and paste text	Highlight the relevant text → click on the Copy icon → place the cursor in the new position → click on the Paste icon.
Find and replace text	Click on the Edit menu → click on Replace → the Find and Replace task pane will be displayed → in the Find what box, enter the word to be replaced → in the Replace with box, enter the new word → click on Replace All → click on OK → click on the cross to close the Find and Replace task pane.
Edit text	Zoom in to the publication → click to place the mouse in the required position → delete the unwanted text → enter the required text.

HOW TO...	METHOD
Format subheadings	Highlight one subheading → click on the Format menu → click on Paragraph → the Paragraph dialogue box will be displayed → click on the drop-down arrow next to Preset and select Flush Left → click on the drop-down arrow next to Alignment and select the required alignment → click on OK → the subheading will remain highlighted → on the Formatting toolbar, click on the drop-down arrow next to the Font box and select a font → in the Font Size box, enter a size and press Enter or select a size from the list.
Copy formatting to subheadings	Highlight the subheading that has been formatted → double-click on the Format Painter icon → highlight the remaining subheadings → press Esc.
Copy formatting to paragraphs of text	Highlight a paragraph that has been formatted as required → double-click on the Format Painter icon → highlight the remaining paragraphs → press Esc.
Balance columns using baseline guides	Highlight all the text → click on the Format menu → click on Paragraph → the Paragraph dialogue box will be displayed → click to place a tick in the box for Align text to baseline guides → click on OK. If the Text in overflow symbol displays or there is still white space → click on Undo and change the Spacing in the Baseline Guides dialogue box. *To change the baseline guides spacing:* Click on the Arrange menu → click on Layout Guides → select the Baseline Guides tab → amend the spacing → click on OK. You may need to try a few settings to achieve column balancing.

For this task you will need the file **burger** from the folder **files_publications**.

1 Create a new single-page publication.

2 a Set up the Master Page or template for the page as follows:

page size	**A4**
page orientation	**portrait/tall**
left margin	**2.85cm**
right margin	**2.85cm**
top margin	**3cm**
bottom margin	**3cm**

   b Enter **your name** in the header and your **centre number** in the footer.

3 a Set up the page layout in a newsletter format, to include a page-wide heading above **two** columns of text:

column widths	**equal**
space between columns	**1.5cm**

   b Draw/display a border around the heading text box.

   c Make sure the border does not touch any text.

4 a Enter the heading **EATING OUT** at the top of the page.

   b Format the heading in a **sans serif** font (e.g. Arial).

   c Make sure the heading text extends across both columns and fills the space across the top of the page. You may increase the character spacing (kerning) and/or font size to achieve this.

   d Make sure there is no more than 1cm of white space to the left or right between the heading and the margins.

5 a Import the image **burger** and place it at the top of the first column below the heading.

   b Make sure there will be no text on either side of the image (set the text wrap). The text in column 1 should begin below the image.

   c The image should not touch the border for the heading area and should not extend into the margin or column space.

6 Save the publication using the filename **fastfd**

For this task you will need the file **mall**. Continue working on the publication **fastfd**.

1 a Import the text file **mall**.

   b The text should begin at the top of the left-hand column below the image **burger**. It should fill the first column then flow under the heading into the second column.

   c Make sure all the text has been imported and is visible on the page.

TIP!

Switch hyphenation off.

2 Format the imported text to be:

   a **left-aligned**

   b in a **sans serif** font that is clearly different from the heading (e.g. Comic Sans MS).

3 a Spell check the text and correct the three spelling errors.

   b Do not make any other amendments to the text file.

4 a Draw a solid line between the two columns of text.

   b The line must begin below the heading frame and extend to the bottom of the page above the footer.

   c Make sure the line does not touch or overlap any text.

   d The line must not extend into any of the margin areas, the header/footer areas or into the heading area. It may touch the border for the heading.

5 a Make sure your publication fits on one page.

   b Check your publication to make sure you have carried out all the instructions correctly.

6 Save your publication keeping the filename **fastfd**

7 Print the publication on one page.

8 Check your printout for accuracy.

You have been asked to make some changes to your publication called **fastfd**.

1   Open the publication and save it using the filename **quick**

2   Change the body text to be **fully justified**.

3   a   Format the body text so that there is one clear line space *after* each paragraph.
    b   Make sure that you do *not* indent the first line of each paragraph.

4   Format the subheadings **Discount Meals**, **Parties** and **Design** as follows.

    a   All the subheadings must be the same size, larger than the body text, but smaller than the heading.
    b   To a **serif** font (e.g. Times New Roman).
    c   To be **centre-aligned**.

5   a   Flip the **burger** image horizontally.
    b   Reduce the size of this image so that it is visibly smaller than it was originally.
    c   Make sure you keep the original proportions of the image.
    d   Move the image to be below the subheading **Discount Meals**
    e   Make sure there is no body text between the image **burger** and the subheading **Discount Meals**
    f   Make sure that the image does not overlap any text or extend into the margin or space between columns.

6   Save your publication keeping the filename **quick**.

Continue working on the publication **quick**.

1   Change the subheading **Design** to **Bright Designs**

2   a   Draw a star shape below the subheading **Bright Designs**

    b   Set the text wrap so there is no text on either side of the shape.

3   a   Balance the columns. You may use any method to achieve this (e.g. amend the text size, leading, kerning and/or image/shape sizes).

    b   Make sure that the heading, subheadings and body text are still three different sizes (large, medium, small).

    c   Make sure all the original text is displayed on one page.

4   Check your publication to make sure you have carried out all the instructions correctly.

5   Save your publication keeping the filename **quick**.

6   Print a copy of the publication on one page.

7   Check your printout for accuracy.

8   Close the publication and exit the software.

You should have the following printouts:

fastfd
quick.

Scenario

You work as an Administrative Assistant for a local primary school. You have been asked to produce an article about a forthcoming activities week and to include information about a school trip.

You will need the files **week**, **active** and **trip** from the folder files_publications.

Task 1

1 Create a new single-page publication.

2 **a** Set up the Master Page or template for the page as follows:

page size	**A4**
page orientation	**portrait/tall**
left margin	**2cm**
right margin	**2cm**
top margin	**2cm**
bottom margin	**2cm**

  b In the bottom margin area, enter **your name**.

3 Set up the page layout in a newsletter format, to include a page-wide heading above **two** columns of text:

column widths   **equal**
space between columns **1cm**

4 **a** Enter the heading **Activities Week** at the top of the page.
  b Format the heading in a **serif** font (e.g. Times New Roman).
  c Make sure the heading text extends across both columns and fills the space across the top of the page. You may increase the character spacing (kerning) and/or font size to achieve this.
  d Make sure there is no more than 1cm of white space to the left or right between the heading and the margins.

5 **a** Import the text file **week**.
  b The text should begin at the top of the left-hand column below the heading. It should fill the first column, then flow under the heading into the second column.
  c Make sure all the text has been imported and is visible on the page.

6 Save the publication using the filename **activity1**

Task 2

Continue working on the publication **activity1**.

1 **a** Import the image **active** and place it at the bottom of the first column.

    b Make sure there will be no text on either side of the image (set the text flow). The text in column 1 should end above the image.

    c Make sure the image fits within column 1.

    d Make sure the image does not touch or overlap any text and does not extend into the margin area or into the column space.

2 Format the imported text to be:

    a **Left-aligned**.

    b In a **serif** font (e.g. Times New Roman).

3 **a** Spell check the text and correct the three spelling errors.

    b Do not make any other amendments to the text file.

4 **a** Import the image **trip**.

    b Place it within the text in the section **Annual School Trip** in the second column.

    c Make sure the image fits within the column.

    d Make sure the image does not overlap any text or extend into the margin or space between columns.

    e Make sure the image is in proportion.

    f Make sure there is no text on either side of the image (set the text flow).

5 **a** Make sure your publication fits on to one page.

    b Check your publication to make sure you have carried out all the instructions correctly.

6 Save your publication keeping the filename **activity1**.

7 Print the publication on one page.

8 Check your printout for accuracy.

Task 3

You have been asked to make some changes to your publication called **activity1**.

1 **a** Crop the **trip** image from the left to remove the child with the blue umbrella. Most of the blue umbrella should be deleted.

  b Move this image so that it is placed more centrally within the column. The image does not need to be precisely centred.

  c Make sure you keep the original proportions of the image and that there is no text on either side of the image.

  d Move the image to be below the subheading **Annual School Trip**

  e Make sure there is no body text between the image **trip** and the subheading **Annual School Trip**

  f Make sure that the image does not overlap any text or extend into the margin or space between columns.

2 Format the subheadings **Uniform and Attendance**, **School Dinners**, **Homework Club**, **Sports** and **Annual School Trip** to be:

  a All the same size, larger than the body text, but smaller than the heading.

  b In a **sans serif** font.

  c **Left aligned**.

3 **a** Draw a line above the heading to separate the top margin area from the text.

  b The line must extend from the left margin to the right margin.

  c Draw a second line below the body text to separate the bottom margin area from the text.

  d The line must extend from the left margin to the right margin.

  e Make sure the lines do not touch or overlap any text or images.

  f The lines must not extend into the left or right margin areas.

4 Save your publication using the new filename **activity2**

Task 4

Continue working on the publication **activity2**.

1   Change the body text to be **fully justified**.

2   **a**   Format the body text so that each paragraph has a **first-line indent**. Do not insert a clear line space between paragraphs.

    b   The subheadings should not be indented.

3   **a**   Amend the publication so that both columns are balanced at the bottom of the page. You may use any method to achieve this (e.g. resize text, amend the kerning or leading, resize images).

    b   Make sure that the heading, subheadings and body text are still three different sizes (large, medium, small).

    c   Make sure all the original text is displayed on one page.

4   Change the subheading **Annual School Trip** to **School Trip**

5   **a**   Check your publication to make sure you have carried out all the instructions correctly.

    b   Make sure the image **trip** is positioned below the subheading **School Trip**

    c   Make sure the image **active** remains positioned at the bottom of column 1.

6   Save your publication keeping the filename **activity2**.

7   Print a copy of the publication on one page.

8   Check your printout for accuracy.

9   Close the publication and exit the software.

You should have the following printouts:
activity1
activity2

Assessment guidelines for Unit 4

- Your tutor will provide you with the file(s) you need to create the publication for the assessment.
- Before an assessment you should create a new folder just for the assessment.

TIP!

Before you start, *copy* the folder containing the files into another user area in case you need to open an original file again.

You are advised to print the text file and to keep it next to you while working on the publication so that:

- you can check that all the text has been imported correctly into your publication
- when you make amendments to the publication, you can check that all the text remains displayed.

Tasks

There will usually be four tasks:

1 You will create a Master Page then, in the publication, you will create a page-wide heading, and enter and format the heading text.

2 You will import the text file and check the spelling. You will also need to import and place image(s), format the text and print the publication.

3 You will make some amendments to the publication (e.g. manipulate the image(s), edit text and draw simple lines/shapes).

4 You will format the body text and subheadings and balance columns. You will print the updated publication.

Create a Master Page and a new publication

- Make sure that you create a new Master Page – do not be tempted to use a previously saved template.
- Make sure that you follow the instructions in the correct order. You must set the paper size first, then the orientation, then the page margins *before* you enter your name in the header/footer. If you amend the margins after you have inserted headers/footers, you will find that the text boxes for the header/footers are not aligned correctly.
- Similarly, if you change the orientation or paper size after inserting headers, you will find that the text boxes are not aligned correctly.
- There will not be a specific instruction to use headers/footers in this unit because some desktop publishing packages do not have this feature. The instruction in the assignment will be similar to 'In the bottom margin area key in your name'. As Publisher does have the facility, you should use a header or footer. Enter your first and last name.

- You do not need to set the margins for the header/footer boxes to zero as the alignment of your name is not assessed. You may use any font size, font type and alignment for your name unless otherwise instructed.

- Although you can create the text boxes for the heading and for the body text on the Master Page, you are advised to switch to Publication view to create the text boxes. This allows you to adjust the height of the heading text box after you have entered and formatted the heading text.

Create the publication

- Create the text box for the heading, and set the text box margins to zero!

- Then enter the heading text. You may use **Best fit**, but check that the heading text extends across the full width of the text box. Use the keyboard techniques you have learnt to increase the font size and/or the character spacing by one point at a time.

- Do not enter the heading in bold unless instructed. It is presented in bold to help you to see what to enter. You may use any font type from the specified font category (sans serif or serif). You do not have to use the font type given in the example.

- Make sure that all the heading text is fully visible on one line in the heading text box. Check the bottom of the text box to make sure the bottom of all letters is fully displayed.

- Adjust the height of the text box as required. If the text is not fully displayed, increase the height. If there is extra space below the text, then reduce the height of the text box.

- Once you are satisfied that you have created the heading text box correctly, entered and formatted the text and adjusted the text box height, *only then* should you create the text box for the main publication.

- Make sure the text boxes do not overlap or that there is no unnecessary gap between the two boxes.

- Make sure both text boxes are positioned on the margin guides. You should not be able to see the blue margin guides once you have inserted the text boxes correctly.

- If a border is displayed around the heading, make sure the border does not touch the text. You may need to change the text box margins (e.g. to 0.1 cm).

Import text and images

- Make sure you create the main text box correctly – align it to the margin guides, the heading text box and the footer text box correctly.

- Make sure you set the text box margins to zero! Then set the number of columns and the space between columns.

- Display the column guides to help you align objects.

- Do take time to set up the publication correctly; it is more time consuming to make adjustments later.

- When you import the text file, zoom into the publication, particularly to the end of the last column, and check that all the text is fully visible on the page. The **Text in overflow** [A⋯] symbol must not be displayed at the end of the page.

- Print the text file and check the printout against the text on the page. You do not need to check all the text – check only the last few lines to make sure that all the text has been imported correctly.

- Make sure the text flows into the columns as instructed.

- Carry out the spell check correctly. Ignore any grammar suggestions and do not change any proper nouns.

- Do not make any unspecified amendments to the text or spacing in the text file.

- Make sure you import the image(s) provided for a particular assessment. Do not be tempted to use your own image(s).

- Make sure the image(s) are placed correctly and that images or shapes do not extend into the column space or margin area. Remember to set the text wrap to top and bottom so that the text does not flow on to the side(s) of the image.

- Format the text in the font category specified (sans serif or serif). Remember, there is no font called serif or sans serif – they are font categories. You may use any font from a category and do not have to use the example given in the assignment (but don't be tempted to experiment with new font types during an assessment!).

- Save your publication using the specified filename. Filenames will not be displayed on the publications. Your tutor will assess this objective.

- You are advised to enter filenames using the same case as in the assignment, but this is not essential. Do not enter a full stop after a filename.

- Always use Print Preview before printing. Use the **Zoom** tool in Print Preview to check your publication.

- You will be instructed to print a composite copy – you should not need to change any settings at this point. Simply print your publication and check that all text, images and headers/footers are displayed on the printout. The images must be clearly displayed on the printouts.

Amend the publication

- Before you begin a task, read through all the instructions. If you need to save the publication with a different filename, then do so before you start the task. This will prevent accidentally saving over the first publication.

- When selecting any text box or image, be careful that you do not accidentally move it as objects can easily move in Publisher.

- Every time you make any amendment, check to make sure the end of the text in the last column is still visible (the **Text in overflow** symbol is not displayed).

- Zoom in to the publication when making any amendments to text so that you can read the text.

- If instructed to find and replace text, make sure that you tick the option for **Find whole words only** and **Match Case**.

- To make column balancing simpler, read through the whole task, edit any text as instructed, then select all the body text, format it, and then format the subheadings. If the columns are still not balanced, use the skills you have learnt to achieve column balancing.

- When you create a drawing feature (e.g. a line or rectangle), use Print Preview to check the position of the drawn object.

- Use text wrap for drawn shapes (except lines).

- Read the instructions carefully to check whether lines should/should not touch other objects. Make sure drawn objects do not extend into the margin or column space unless otherwise instructed.

- Make sure that images do not extend into the column space or margin space unless otherwise instructed. Make sure that no images are distorted.

- Remember to use Print Preview before you print the final publication. Then check the printouts again. You will usually have two printouts for this unit.

- The printouts do not need to be in colour – black-and-white prints are acceptable.

- Measure the top, bottom, left and right margins with a ruler on the first printout. If any margins are incorrect on the printout, check the margins and the **Paper Size** in the **Page Setup** and dialogue box. If these are correct ask your tutor to check the printer settings.

Good luck!

Index

chicken & mushroom pie

1. preheat oven to **200°C.**

1.017

2. finely chop 1 **onion** & 2 cloves of **garlic**.

cut 4 **chicken** breasts into bite-sized chunks & quarter **200g button mushrooms**.

3. fry chicken in 1tbsp olive **oil** over medium heat until seared.

add **mushrooms** & continue to fry until chicken is **golden brown.** set aside in baking dish.

4. fry onion & garlic in 1tbsp olive **oil** until soft.

add to chicken & mushrooms.

5. melt **50g butter** in saucepan.

stir in **2tbsp** plain **flour** to form a smooth thick paste.

6. slowly add **2tsp** dried **tarragon,** salt & pepper, **284ml milk,** & **150ml chicken stock.**

stirring well, **simmer** until thickened. pour over set aside ingredients & mix well.

7. place 1 sheet of ready-made **puff pastry** on top of contents of dish & bake in oven for **20-25mins** until pastry is golden brown.

chicken, leek, & bacon crumble

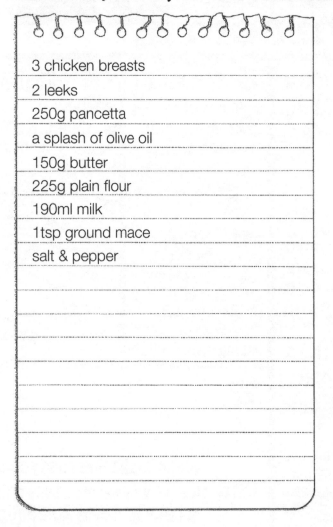

3 chicken breasts

2 leeks

250g pancetta

a splash of olive oil

150g butter

225g plain flour

190ml milk

1tsp ground mace

salt & pepper